# HUMAN RESOURCE DEVELOPMENT QUARTERLY

## Sponsored by ASTD and the
## Academy of Human Resource Development

VOLUME 16      SPRING 2005      NUMBER 1

*Human Resource Development Quarterly* (print ISSN 1044-8004; online ISSN 1532-1096 at www.interscience.wiley.com) is published quarterly by Wiley Subscription Services, Inc., A Wiley Company, at Jossey-Bass, 989 Market Street, San Francisco, CA 94103-1741, and is sponsored by ASTD and the Academy of Human Resource Development.

MICROFILM copies of issues and articles are available in 16mm and 35mm, as well as microfiche in 105mm, through University Microfilms Inc., 300 North Zeeb Road, Ann Arbor, Michigan 48106-1346.

*Human Resource Development Quarterly* is indexed in Anbar Abstracts, Business Education Index, Current Index to Journals in Education (ERIC), Sociological Abstracts, and Up-to-Date Publications.


*Human Resource Development Quarterly* is published in one volume of four issues a year, appearing in March, June, September, and December. Subscription rates: for institutions, agencies, and libraries, $235 in the United States, $275 in Canada and Mexico, $279 in the rest of the world; for individuals, $85 in the United States, Canada, and Mexico, and $109 in the rest of the world. To ensure correct and prompt delivery, all orders must give either the name of an individual or an official purchase order number.

SUBSCRIPTION ORDERS should be mailed to Customer Service, Jossey-Bass, 989 Market Street, San Francisco, CA 94103-1741, or phone (888) 378-2537. *Change-of-address* notifications should provide the subscriber's old and new address. *Missing copies* will be replaced if valid claims are received within 90 days from date of mailing.

EDITORIAL CORRESPONDENCE may be sent via e-mail to the Editor, Darlene F. Russ-Eft, at zmresearch@aol.com, or to the Managing Editor, Laura Boehme, at boehmel@onid.orst.edu.

COVER ART BY WILLI BAUM.

www.josseybass.com

# AHRD Officers and Board of Directors

# Manuscript Reviewers

As a refereed journal, *Human Resource Development Quarterly* depends on qualified individuals to serve as manuscript reviewers. Reviewers have a unique way of contributing to the HRD field in that they help determine the quality and nature of the research. Reviewers should expect to receive approximately four manuscripts per volume, although the number may vary depending on the type of manuscripts received and the individual reviewer's expertise. Personal feedback is given to reviewers at the conclusion of each volume.

Individuals who wish to be considered as manuscript reviewers should take the following actions:

- Submit a complete curriculum vitae, listing educational background, professional employment, publications and presentations, service to other journals, and any other relevant information.
- Include a statement describing specific areas of HRD expertise, such as cost-benefit analysis, training transfer, or organizational learning.
- Include a statement describing specific areas of research expertise, such as qualitative methods, ANOVA, or multivariate analysis.

The editor reviews these materials on a continuous basis, so individuals should receive immediate notification of their status as a reviewer. Materials should be sent to Laura A. Boehme, Managing Editor, HRDQ, Oregon State University, School of Education, 421 Education Hall, Corvallis, OR 97331. E-mail address: boehmel@onid.orst.edu.

# ACKNOWLEDGMENT OF FINANCIAL SUPPORT

The editors and Editorial Board gratefully acknowledge the financial support given to *Human Resource Development Quarterly* by corporations and organizations. This support helps make it possible to maintain the standards of quality required of a scholarly journal.

### The following are acknowledged as supporters of HRDQ:

**OREGON STATE UNIVERSITY**
Corvallis, OR

**AMERICAN INSTITUTES FOR RESEARCH**
Palo Alto, California

# CONTENTS

REVIEW

# Research Integrity: Ensuring Trust in the Academy

The reputation of the academy stems at least partially from published research. This reputation requires that research be ethically conducted and reported such that scholars, consumers, and the public have faith in the academy. Thus, trust is the catalyst that ensures our reputation as individual scholar-practitioners and as a profession.

How do we ensure that our published research can be trusted? What constrains or influences researcher behaviors? And what guidelines should we use to ensure trust and research integrity? Before I address these questions, it is important to clarify what I mean by *integrity* and *trust*.

## Defining Integrity and Trust

It should come as no surprise that integrity shows up in religious doctrine, in the Bible, the Koran, and the Torah, for example. But the word *integrity* also is used in many human resource development–related documents. For example, integrity is mentioned throughout the Academy of Human Resource Development Standards on Ethics and Integrity, in the ASTD and ISPI Codes of Ethics, and in numerous editorials and articles published in HRD-related journals. But what are we really talking about when we use the word *integrity*? According to *Webster's Unabridged Dictionary* (1983), integrity is "the quality or state of being of sound moral principle; uprightness, honesty, and sincerity."

Integrity is a virtuous character trait that is closely connected to reliability, trustworthiness, honesty, and having principles. A person who has integrity can be counted on to be consistent and harmonious; someone who does not is fickle and discordant. May (1996) says that integrity has three aspects: coherence of value orientation, mature development of a critical point of view, and disposition to act in a principled way. Warren Bennis is credited with saying that integrity is the basis of trust. Without integrity there is no trust. Going to *Webster* (1983) again, to paraphrase, trust is a reliance on the integrity, veracity, justice, friendship, or other sound principle of another person [or group of people]. In research, trust has been shown to be related to variables such as reward practices and intent to leave an organization or profession. Without trust, individuals and organizations suffer.

Professions such as HRD nurture trust through self-policing. Self-policing keeps government regulation at bay while leaving the governance and canon of the profession to members whose livelihood depends on the integrity of the profession. Without self-policing, integrity and trust are eroded. Even with self-policing, research integrity is currently running a distant second to the pressures of productivity and other influences on researchers.

## Influences on Researchers

Researchers and others who develop and use data are under more pressures now than ever before to produce. Public criticism of higher education and corporations has reached a fever pitch. Higher education has evolved (or devolved) into competitive sparring, where scholars' academic power and prestige is measured not by teaching or collegiality but by revenue generated. Compared with education and the humanities and even in professional colleges such as business, the federal sponsorship of research has changed the balance and influence of research. This change in the research landscape has affected how we see ourselves and how we are seen by learners, colleagues, and other stakeholders.

The HRD academy is certainly not immune to growing elitism in academia. We are being forced to convert from seekers of truth to seekers of revenue. Part of this landscape is the "social and economic barriers that are separating the humanists from the scientists in an era that demands that issues be examined from a multidisciplinary perspective" (Kennedy & Katz, 1995, p. 34). This exacerbates our ability to conduct multidisciplinary research so desperately needed in increasingly global work environments.

The new implied contract in academia has profound implications for research integrity. As superstar scientists bring massive projects with huge revenues, big laboratories, and new confidentiality and conflicts-of-interest agreements, an environment of fast and loose disguised as innovation is nurtured. It is axiomatic that if researchers are not upholding integrity in their research, then unethical behaviors are being rewarded by someone or something. If our reputation is governed by integrity as I have suggested, then we must look beyond academia to the academy and address what responsibilities it has to ensure trust in our research.

There are no universally recognized sets of standards defining appropriate and inappropriate moral conduct within academic or corporate research environments. The closest we come to standards are codes of ethics and regulations for investigators involved in federally funded projects. Whether we are in a university engaged in empirical research, a nonprofit involved in qualitative data analysis, or a corporation doing action research, as a research community we should assume responsibility for monitoring our own research integrity. If we are to become a profession equal to recognized professions like accounting or medicine, we must acknowledge that the public makes little distinction between drug research and research on training transfer when it comes to trust and integrity. The public expects research to be valid and truthful. As Macrina (2000) suggested, "The public regards science as the definitive vehicle for uncovering truth. They cannot understand how scientific facts can be disputed" (p. 2).

Finally, researchers base their behaviors on tacit or implied knowledge or assumptions that may not be ethically correct in every case. Background, ethnicity, family and life experiences, culture, and environment establish in us a particular set of views concerning right and wrong. Codes of ethics and other guidelines demonstrate core values and the intentions of the profession that underwrite them. Unfortunately, not everyone understands and agrees with the moral assumptions on which such standards are based. The assumption that everyone who claims membership in the academy understands the concepts of protection of human subjects, confidentiality, and conflict of interest is less true than we might imagine. A professional moral consensus simply does not exist. I doubt that even those who profess to understand ethical guidelines completely understand or fully appreciate the supporting philosophical and practical assumptions and arguments. I believe this lack of knowledge is influencing how some researchers react in stressful and ethically conflicting situations.

Expanding the frontiers of scientific inquiry in HRD does not justify unethical conduct of research. Although I would be surprised if anyone reading this editorial would accept that not protecting human participants or cooking the books by manipulating data outweighs the benefits derived from research, I do believe that without stated guidelines and periodic prompts and reminders, researchers may overlook their responsibilities or be unaware of the environments that constrain or control behaviors that influence the integrity of their research.

## Guidance for HRD Research Integrity

I look at three primary ethical principles that have the potential to ensure the integrity of HRD research: (1) respect for persons, beneficence, and justice; (2) guidelines on conflicts of interest and conscience; and (3) activities of peer review.

No doubt, processes like institutional review boards (IRBs) and human subjects protections are familiar to researchers employed by federally funded institutions. However, it is important to remind all scholars and practitioners, whether in a university, a think tank, or a corporation, of the importance of the principles under which such rules and regulations rest. A better awareness and understanding of these principles and guidelines might also help new faculty just starting institutional research and especially for those doing research in corporate or in some international settings where few formal guidelines, regulations or standards exist or where enforcement is minimal.

The three primary ethical principles HRD research should address are respect for persons, beneficence, and justice. In addition, we must address issues of conflicts of interests. Within universities and other federally funded organizations, these principles are institutionalized under the Belmont Report, a statement of basic ethical principles that includes respect for persons, beneficence, and justice.[1]

Respect for persons is carried out through protection of human subjects as research participants. We must be the guardians and guarantors of the protection of the participants in our research, beginning with their knowledgeable, voluntary, and informed consent. The principle of respect for persons means that people must be considered autonomous agents, and anyone with diminished autonomy must be entitled to protections. The way this principle is carried out is through informed consent. This means that people must be given the opportunity to choose what happens to them. It includes the giving of information on the research and must include a way to ensure that people really understand the research. It also includes the right of a person not to participate and be assured that nothing adverse will happen to him or her by declining to participate or dropping out of the research at any time.

The principle of beneficence means no harm to people and that the research should maximize benefits and minimize potential harm to subjects. For the participant, this means that these benefits and harms must be clearly understood and accepted. Compared to research in the hard sciences and medicine, the conduct of HRD-related research in most cases presents minimal risks to participants. It is unlikely (but not impossible) that participants would die or be seriously injured as a result of an HRD intervention. But there are risks and potential harms that we should not overlook or take lightly; loss of privacy and loss of ownership of intellectual property are two examples. These and other similar risks must be made clear to participants.

Finally, the principle of justice means that harms and benefits cannot be given to just a small group; it must be distributed fairly, and people must be aware of how participants are selected or not selected.

Guidelines for conflicts of interest assist the researcher, especially when assuming more than one role. A conflict of interest exists when a professional is tempted to (or actually carries out) compromise professional judgment for financial or personal gain and may cause the professional's integrity to be questioned, betray a trust, or cause negative outcomes for himself or herself or others. Of course, we are subject to conflicting demands all the time. Most of these are handled by subscribing to the norms of the research or professional community. Conflicts of conscience occur when researchers with deeply held beliefs find themselves having to make judgments about research whose very nature is unacceptable or in opposition to strong beliefs. The outcome is that personal convictions take precedence over scientific merit.

One of the most important activities available to us to ensure integrity is peer review. As a source of ethical and professional conduct, peer review is a means to apply ethics through shared governance. Beyond the walls of academia, the tradition of self-governance through peer review builds professional competence and trust among peers.

Peer review works because it can screen for weaknesses and inadequacies in design, method, or interpretation of results, yet it cannot absolutely ensure that misconduct does not occur. For us to provide scholars and practitioners with opportunities to create ethical research, integrity must be woven into all of the behaviors that make up research, from conception to interpretation.

## Implications for HRD Research and Practice

HRD scholars and scholar-practitioners are expected to exhibit a higher degree of integrity and adhere to a more stringent set of ethical behaviors around research than other related professions. As we continue to provide results of research that enables individual and organizational growth and to provide for professional development, we must be a model of responsible research in order to maintain credibility and trust. Ethical boundaries established by the profession, academia, and federal regulations are constantly being tested by researchers as a result of personal agendas and external pressures. Thus, ensuring research integrity in such a contentious environment must involve a clear focus on the interaction between individual, the organization, and professional intention.

### Note

1. The National Research Act of 1974 codified the requirement that human subjects in research must be protected and set the stage for the issuance of the Belmont Report. Due to publicity from the infamous Tuskegee Syphilis Study, the National Research Act was passed to identify the basic ethical principles that should underlie the conduct of biomedical and behavioral research on humans. The Tuskegee study involved the injection by the U.S. Public Health Service of some four hundred low-income African Americans with syphilis. These uninformed subjects were monitored for forty years, until 1972. Although they received free medical examinations, they were never told about their disease. And although a proven cure was available in the 1950s (penicillin), the study continued with participants being denied treatment. Many participants died, and many more suffered the ravages of the disease. The study was finally stopped in 1973, but only after its existence was publicized and it became a political embarrassment. The National Research Act created a commission that later developed the 1979 Belmont Report (U.S. Department of Health and Human Services, 1979). Most current regulations, including the Food and Drug Administration and National Institutes of Health regulations and Codes of Federal Regulations (CFRs) are based on the Belmont Report. 45 CRF 46, called the Common Rule, includes requirements for ensuring compliance by research institutes like universities; requirements for researchers (like doctoral students and professors) in obtaining and documenting informed consent; requirements for IRB membership, function, operations, review processes, and record keeping; and additional requirements for certain vulnerable subjects, such as children and prisoners.

## References

Kennedy, V. W., & Katz, R. N. (1995). Integrity in the research university. *SRA Journal, 27,* 33–38.

Macrina, F. L. (2000). *Scientific integrity: An introductory text with cases.* Washington, DC: ASM Press.

May, L. (1996). *The socially responsive self: Social theory and professional ethics.* Chicago: University of Chicago Press.

U.S. Department of Health and Human Services. (1979). *The Belmont Report: Ethical principles for the protection of human subjects of research.* Washington, DC: U.S. Government Printing Office.

*Webster's unabridged dictionary.* (1983). Springfield, MA: Merriam-Webster.

TIM HATCHER
NORTH CAROLINA STATE UNIVERSITY

# Outsourcing Relationships Between Firms and Their Training Providers: The Role of Trust

*Thomas W. Gainey, Brian S. Klaas*

*Firms increasingly use external vendors to provide training for their employees. And because trust has been found to be essential in successful interfirm relationships, this study identified a number of factors thought to be associated with both self-interested trust and socially oriented trust between firms and their training suppliers. Using data obtained from 323 organizations, regression analysis suggests that idiosyncratic training, program uncertainty, vendor dependency, contractual specificity, and communication accuracy and frequency were significantly related to higher levels of trust in outsourcing relationships.*

Outsourcing human resource (HR) activities traditionally performed in-house is becoming increasingly common (Lepak & Snell, 1998). In fact, research suggests that 93 percent of HR departments outsource at least some of their work (Greer, Youngblood, & Gray, 1999). And while a number of HR activities have been targeted for outsourcing, training is one functional area where outsourcing is especially prevalent (Bassi, Cheney, & Van Buren, 1997). However, although organizations spend more than $54 billion each year on the design and delivery of training (Industry Report, 2000) and given that training and development activities are often linked to strategic issues within the firm (Huselid, Jackson, & Schuler, 1997; Wright & Snell, 1998), little research has examined outsourcing in this important HR area.

Anecdotal evidence suggests wide variation across firms in the degree to which the outsourcing of training has yielded the desired results (Kaeter, 1995; Baker, 1996; Laabs, 1993). And while limited empirical research exists within the HR literature to help practitioners understand conditions that tend to lead to more positive outcomes, the outsourcing literature in general provides some guidance. In particular, the trust that develops between firms and their suppliers consistently emerges as an important factor in successful outsourcing relationships (Adler, 2003; Child, 2001). In fact, a lack of trust has been identified as the major cause for failure across a number of outsourcing contexts (Niederkofler, 1991; Moore, 1998; Logan, 2000). Some researchers even argue that trust between partners is the essential element in successful interfirm relations (Zeffane, 1995).

Given that trust has proven to be such an important factor in interfirm successes (Child, 2001; Swan, Trawick, Rink, & Roberts, 1988; Zaheer, McEvily, & Perrone, 1998) and that trust is an area that can be developed and nurtured by management (Zeffane, 1995), this study sought to identify factors that are necessary to building and maintaining trusting relations with training vendors.

## Theory and Hypotheses

Trust is commonly described as an expectation that another party will not act in an opportunistic manner (Bradach & Eccles, 1989). Implicit in this definition is the element of choice. Luhmann (1988) contends that if there is no choice and one must simply surrender to the more powerful or influential partner, the belief that one will not act opportunistically is simply a matter of hope, not trust. Thus, trust requires a conscious decision to reveal a certain degree of vulnerability to another party (Nooteboom, 1996).

A review of the literature reveals that trust can assume many different forms and may be affected by a number of factors within the context of interpersonal relations (Kramer, 1996). Indeed, a number of researchers have proposed different dimensions of trust and have attached a variety of labels to identify them (Gulati, 1995; Lyons & Mehta, 1997; Nooteboom, 1996). However, within the literature, two basic types of trust have consistently been identified: self-interested trust and socially oriented trust.

Self-interested trust is described as having basic economic underpinnings where the costs and benefits of behaving trustworthy are calculative and measurable (Dasgupta, 1988). Therefore, there are incentives to behave in a trustworthy manner because the possible negative consequences of opportunistic behavior far exceed any potential benefits (Lyons & Mehta, 1997). Thus, organizations can be relied on only to the extent to which they feel their behavior will somehow have a direct impact on future returns (Sheppard & Tuchinsky, 1996). For instance, in outsourcing relationships, it is possible that deceit on the part of the vendor could lead to a damaged reputation or loss of future business. Thus, for self-interested trust, the propensity to trust might be equated to an impersonal cost-benefit decision.

Whereas self-interested trust denotes more of a short-term, impersonal orientation, socially oriented trust focuses more on the ongoing social factors in a relationship. That is, partners can be expected to refrain from opportunism because of established norms of behavior or a sense of duty, personal loyalty, and devotion to the other (Lyons & Mehta, 1997). At this stage, parties develop strong norms about how activities will be handled, clear expectations regarding performance levels, and the ability to accurately predict each other's behavior. As they gain experience with one another, they develop a higher level of confidence in each other's ability to perform in a consistent, professional manner. Interestingly, unlike self-interested trust, socially oriented trust provides some leeway in relationships. For instance, if a party engages in a questionable activity and is able to provide a reasonable explanation for the behavior, the other party is more likely to disregard the incident and continue with the relationship.

In summary, trust might best be envisioned as an evolutionary process that develops as it progresses from its self-interested stage to its more advanced socially oriented stage. In fact, Lewicki and Bunker (1996) equate trust building to gardening. They suggest that as you till the soil each year, you come to understand which vegetables grow in the sandy sections and which in the moist sections. Similarly, socially oriented trust evolves only after parties cultivate their knowledge of each other by observing behaviors over time. In this study, we draw on the trust literature to suggest a number of factors that are potentially related to both self-interested and socially oriented trust between firms and their external training providers.

**Idiosyncratic Training.** Certain programs are outsourced that might be considered off-the-shelf training. That is, a training vendor might design a program and then deliver it, with few changes, to numerous customers. While this training will likely not result in a competitive advantage for a firm, neither does it significantly increase the potential for opportunistic actions by either party. Vendors are able to spread their costs over many customers, and firms typically experience lower costs due to economies of scale.

Alternatively, when training is idiosyncratic, or tailored to a particular firm, the customer or the vendor, or both parties, will likely be required to invest resources to design and deliver the training. However, because the training is of little value in other contexts, it is of great interest to the party (or parties) that has (have) invested the resources that the relationship continues. Therefore, while primarily economically motivated, parties who have made substantial investments often behave in a trustworthy manner to ensure long-term associations with their trading partners (Lewicki & Bunker, 1996). It is also possible that seemingly altruistic behaviors and amiable actions that are exhibited to ensure continued relations may be positively received and reciprocated by the other party, thus forming the basis for more socially oriented trust (Lewicki & Bunker, 1996). Therefore, idiosyncratic training will lead to higher levels of both self-interested and socially-oriented trust:

HYPOTHESIS 1. *There will be a positive relationship between the degree to which a firm is outsourcing idiosyncratic training and the level of both self-interested and socially oriented trust with that firm's training vendors.*

**Program Uncertainty.** Many training suppliers offer standard programs. They have been designed and are delivered in such a way that each customer that purchases the service essentially receives the same materials and instruction. Here, the requirements and expectations are well known by both parties, the content and costs can generally be agreed on in advance by each party, and the results of the training can often be assessed through standardized exams or improvements in various performance measures.

With other training programs, vendors must often be granted a certain latitude in either the design or the delivery of training, or, in other cases, it may be difficult to objectively evaluate the overall impact of the training. Here, the uncertainty creates the potential for opportunistic behavior by the vendor, and it is likely that firms will view vendors who have substantial discretion with skepticism (Williamson, 1975). Therefore, where there is substantial uncertainty related to the design and delivery of training, not only will lower levels of self-interested trust be observed, but the ambiguity makes it more difficult for socially oriented trust to form and evolve.

HYPOTHESIS 2. *There will be a negative relationship between the degree to which the design and delivery of training is uncertain and the level of both self-interested and socially oriented trust with that firm's training vendors.*

**Vendor Dependency.** Due to a small market base, substantial investments, or limited resources, it is possible for training vendors to become overly reliant on one particular customer. When this occurs, it is likely that the supplier will recognize that the potential benefits of acting in a trustworthy manner far exceed the benefits of acting in a self-interested way (Lyons & Mehta, 1997; Ring & Van de Ven, 1992). Therefore, vendors might be inclined to be more accommodating to customers (Nooteboom, 1996) and to demonstrate high levels of commitment to a customer's values and beliefs (Lewicki & Bunker, 1996), both foundations on which socially oriented trust is established (Kramer, 1993). Thus, while these actions may initially be purely economically motivated and increase self-interested trust, higher levels of socially oriented trust may ultimately result as well:

HYPOTHESIS 3. *There will be a positive relationship between the degree to which vendors are dependent on a firm's business and the level of both self-interested and socially oriented trust with that firm's training vendors.*

*Outsourcing Knowledge, Skills, and Abilities.* As managers gain experience in dealing with outside vendors, they will develop and refine their outsourcing-related knowledge, skills, and abilities (KSAs) (Borthick, 2001). Specifically, they should become more adept at identifying competent training vendors, negotiating mutually advantageous agreements, and evaluating vendors' effectiveness (Harkins, Brown, & Sullivan, 1995; Takeishi, 2001). Thus, where both the customer and the vendor possess relatively clear understandings about training needs and expected results, the potential for opportunistic behavior substantially decreases, resulting in the potential for higher levels of self-interested trust. In addition, this mutual understanding creates a favorable environment in which socially oriented trusting relations can be established and maintained.

HYPOTHESIS 4. *There will be a positive relationship between the degree to which those in a firm possess outsourcing-related KSAs and the level of both self-interested and socially oriented trust with that firm's training vendors.*

*Contractual Specificity.* Typically, when training is outsourced, an agreement is signed between the customer and the vendor. For standard off-the-shelf training, the contractual agreement may simply outline the date, time, and cost of the training. In these cases, there is little room for disagreement or for one party to behave in a self-interested way. Therefore, one might expect higher levels of self-interested trust to develop.

Conversely, when training becomes more involved or is tailored to a particular customer, the potential for misunderstandings and self-serving actions increases. In turn, the ability to establish trusting relations is greatly reduced because parties must devote greater efforts and resources to protecting their interests. However, contractual agreements may act to mitigate these unfavorable conditions. Specifically, where contracts have undergone sufficient development, negotiation, and review (Aubert, Rivard, & Patry, 1996; Shelanski & Klein, 1995), customers and vendors can be relatively confident that each party will meet the obligations set forth in the formal agreement. Thus, efforts can be directed toward building relationships rather than monitoring the other party's behavior, resulting in higher levels of socially oriented trust:

HYPOTHESIS 5. *There will be a positive relationship between the degree to which a firm's outsourcing contracts contain detailed specifications and the level of both self-interested and socially oriented trust with that firm's training vendors.*

*Communication Accuracy and Frequency.* The linkage between communication behaviors and trust has received considerable attention from organizational researchers (Anderson & Weitz, 1989; Mishra, 1996). In general, it is believed that accurate and frequent communication is essential to building levels of trust in interfirm alliances (Shapiro, Sheppard, & Cheraskin, 1992; Anderson, Lodish, & Weitz, 1987). Certainly, precise and regular communication between the firm and its training supplier greatly reduces opportunities for one party to take advantage of the other, resulting in higher levels of self-interested trust. However, it might be socially oriented trust that is most affected by accurate and frequent exchanges.

For trust to evolve to higher forms, it is essential that the quality of information provided by each party be preserved (Daft & Lengel, 1986; Devlin & Bleackley, 1988). If customers and vendors fail to establish communication processes that permit the accurate exchange of messages or if they conceal important information, there is reasonable doubt that trusting relations will emerge. In addition, when parties regularly exchange information about their basic processes, capabilities, and ambitions, not only do they reduce the potential for misunderstandings and ambiguity, they also begin to develop intense, meaningful relationships. This insight and knowledge provide an important basis for socially oriented trust to evolve (McAllister, 1995):

HYPOTHESIS 6. *There will be a positive relationship between the accuracy with which a firm communicates with its training vendors and the level of both self-interest and socially oriented trust with that firm's training vendors.*

HYPOTHESIS 7. *There will be a positive relationship between the frequency with which a firm communicates with its training vendors and the level of both self-interested and socially oriented trust with that firm's training vendors.*

## Methods

Here we look at the sample and the measures used in this study.

*Sample.* The sample for this study was obtained from the membership list of the American Society for Training and Development (ASTD). All ASTD members in the United States who identified themselves as either training managers or training directors were selected to participate. All of these 1,361 individuals were mailed a survey designed to assess attributes of their training programs, characteristics of their firm, features of their contractual agreements, and the nature of the relationship with their training suppliers. We elected to use only training managers and directors in this study because we felt that they would be the most likely individuals within an organization to have the necessary insights and information regarding their firm's training activities to respond to our survey. Although the ASTD membership list had a variety of additional job titles listed (including consultants and educators), we did not think that these job titles indicated that they would be responsible for training within their firms.

Prior to the mailing, the survey was examined by three outside faculty members and three HR professionals to ensure that the items in it were reasonable and did not ask the participants overly intrusive questions or present any ethical dilemmas. Respondents were asked to mail the surveys directly back to the researchers in an enclosed business-reply envelope and were guaranteed that all data would be kept in strict confidence.

Although all ASTD members who identified themselves as training managers or training directors were included in this sample, we asked individuals to complete and return the survey only if their organization outsourced some or all of the design and delivery of their training and if they were the individuals responsible for managing these outsourcing relationships. This was necessary because only firms that actually had outsourcing experience could complete the survey items and because we realized that individuals other than the training professionals might be responsible for obtaining and monitoring outside suppliers who provided training-related services to the organization.

Respondents returned 323 of the 1,361 surveys, resulting in a response rate of 24 percent. However, it is likely that at least some of the 1,361 training professionals who were mailed the survey declined to participate either because their firm did not outsource any of its training or because the training professional was not the individual responsible for managing the outsourcing relationship with external suppliers.

To determine if there was a nonresponse bias, as a result of the restrictions we placed on participants, we then compared the 323 respondents to the 1,361 training professionals who were initially mailed surveys on the basis of their industry classification. We used industry classification because this was the only variable that we had for both respondents and the overall sample. To test for nonresponse bias, we compared (using a $t$-test) the percentage of respondents in a particular industry to the percentage of the overall sample in that same industry across the following industrial classifications: manufacturing, food, health, financial, transportation, utilities, hospitality, and retail. No significant differences were observed between respondents and the overall sample in any of the industry classifications. Thus, at least in terms of industry classification, no response bias was observed.

**Measures.** Because there has been little empirical work dealing specifically with outsourced training, existing measures for the variables in this study were not available. Instead, measures were developed by modifying items from related areas and developing new items.

To establish the validity of the constructs, the individual survey items were subjected to an exploratory factor analysis. The article appendix presents the measures, their component items, and the results of the factor analysis.

*Dependent Variables.* In the literature, trust has been conceptualized at a variety of levels (Rousseau, Sitkin, Burt, & Camerer, 1998). For instance, empirical research has examined trust at the individual level (McCauley & Kuhnert, 1992), the team level (Webber, 2002), and the organizational level of analysis (Zaheer et al., 1998). In this study, three items were used to assess both Self-Interested Trust (alpha = .70) and Socially Oriented Trust (alpha = .84) at the organizational level. The items used to measure self-interested trust were designed to determine the extent to which training suppliers had acted in self-serving ways, whereas the socially oriented trust items focused on the extent to which there was a sense of loyalty and responsibility in the relationship.

*Independent Variables.* Training managers responded to a number of items pertaining to the nature of their training programs. The degree to which training was tailored to their organization was assessed using three items (Idiosyncratic Training, alpha = .73). The degree to which training suppliers had substantial latitude in designing and delivering the training was also measured using three items (Program Uncertainty, alpha = .80).

Using four items, training managers were asked to consider the degree to which their training suppliers were dependent on them for business (Vendor Dependency, alpha = .86), the degree to which managers in their own firm had acquired outsourcing-related KSAs (Outsourcing KSAs, alpha = .83), and characteristics of their contractual agreements with training vendors (Contractual Specificity, alpha = .87).

Finally, the accuracy and frequency of communication with training vendors were measured with two items (Communication Accuracy, alpha = .88) and three items (Communication Frequency, alpha = .93), respectively.

*Control Variable.* Given the organizational-level nature of this study, we also asked about the number of individuals employed by the firm. It is possible that the size of the firm might influence the number and types of training programs used and thus the nature of the relationship between organizations and their outside training providers.

*Data Analysis.* Multiple regression analysis was used to test the proposed relationships in this study. Specifically, two models were tested. In the first model, Self-Interested Trust served as the dependent variable, and in the second model, Socially Oriented Trust was the dependent measure.

## Results

Table 1 reports the means and standard deviations as well as the correlation matrix for the variables. There are several significant correlations among the independent variables. Thus, we formally tested for the presence of multicollinearity by examining the variance inflation factor (VIF) for each independent variable. Any VIF value over 10.0 normally indicates that multicollinearity may be unduly affecting the least-squares estimates (Neter, Wasserman, & Kutner, 1990). Our largest VIF was 1.71, suggesting that multicollinearity was not a problem.

## Table 1. Descriptive Statistics and Correlations

| | Mean | SD | 1 | 2 | 3 | 4 | 5 | 6 | 7 | 8 | 9 |
|---|---|---|---|---|---|---|---|---|---|---|---|
| 1. Self-Interested Trust | 3.26 | .76 | | | | | | | | | |
| 2. Socially Oriented Trust | 3.36 | .70 | .46** | | | | | | | | |
| 3. Idiosyncratic Training | 3.02 | .82 | .21** | .26** | | | | | | | |
| 4. Program Uncertainty | 2.39 | .71 | -.30** | -.20** | -.03 | | | | | | |
| 5. Vendor Dependency | 2.74 | .79 | .02 | .21** | .23** | .14* | | | | | |
| 6. Outsourcing KSAs | 2.81 | .83 | .18** | .31** | .21** | -.10 | .12* | | | | |
| 7. Contractual Specificity | 3.37 | .81 | .38** | .36** | .27** | -.33** | .02 | .29** | | | |
| 8. Communication Accuracy | 3.78 | .58 | .28** | .51** | .05 | -.19** | .08 | .25** | .27** | | |
| 9. Communication Frequency | 3.23 | .93 | .29** | .59** | .32** | -.09 | .22** | .44** | .36** | .45** | |
| 10. Firm Size | 2,336 | 6,199 | -.04 | -.01 | .09 | .02 | .00 | .03 | .03 | -.04 | .06 |

Note: N ranges from 324 to 329.

*$p < .05$. **$p < .01$.

Table 2 presents the regression equations. The results show that the Self-Interested Trust model had an $R^2$ of .22 and that the Socially Oriented Trust model had an $R^2$ of .47. The $F$ values for both equations are statistically significant ($p < .01$). In addition, the estimations for these models reveal support for a majority of the hypothesized relationships.

In hypothesis 1, we predicted that more idiosyncratic training would be positively associated with the dependent measures. While the coefficient for Idiosyncratic Training was significantly related ($p < .01$) to Self-Interested Trust, the relationship between Idiosyncratic Training and Socially Oriented Trust was not significant.

Hypothesis 2 suggested that as uncertainty associated with the design and delivery of training increased, the development of trust would be inhibited. As proposed, Program Uncertainty was negatively and significantly related to both Self-Interest Trust ($p < .01$) and Socially Oriented Trust ($p < .05$).

We predicted in hypothesis 3 that the more reliant vendors were on the firm, the more likely it was that trusting relations would emerge. Results showed that the coefficient for Vendor Dependency was neither significantly related to Self-Interested Trust, nor in the predicted direction. However, Vendor Dependency was significantly related to Socially Oriented Trust ($p < .05$).

Hypothesis 4 suggested that higher levels of outsourcing-related KSAs would be associated with higher levels of trust. But Outsourcing KSAs was not significantly related to either Self-Interested Trust or Socially Oriented Trust.

### Table 2. Regression Analyses

| Dependent Variables | Self-Interested Trust | | Socially Oriented Trust | |
|---|---|---|---|---|
| | $b^a$ | SE | $b^a$ | SE |
| Independent variables | | | | |
| Hypothesis 1: Idiosyncratic Training | .11* | .05 | .08 | .04 |
| Hypothesis 2: Program Uncertainty | −.17** | .06 | −.09* | .05 |
| Hypothesis 3: Vendor Dependency | −.01 | .05 | .09* | .04 |
| Hypothesis 4: Outsourcing KSAs | −.01 | .05 | .02 | .04 |
| Hypothesis 5: Contractual Specificity | .22** | .06 | .09* | .04 |
| Hypothesis 6: Communication Accuracy | .11* | .08 | .27** | .06 |
| Hypothesis 7: Communication Frequency | .12* | .06 | .39** | .04 |
| Control variable | | | | |
| Firm size | −.05 | .00 | −.03 | .00 |
| $R^2$ | .22 | | .47 | |
| $F$ | 10.42 | | 31.76 | |
| $N$ | 297 | | 297 | |

[a]Standardized beta coefficients.

*$p < .05$. **$p < .01$.

Hypothesis 5 proposed that more detailed contractual arrangements would be associated with higher levels of trust between firms and their external training suppliers. The significant and positive relationship between Contractual Specificity and Self-Interested Trust ($p < .01$) and between Contractual Specificity and Socially Oriented Trust ($p < .05$) lends support to this prediction.

As predicted in hypothesis 6, a positive and significant ($p < .01$) relationship was also found between Communication Accuracy and Self-Interested Trust ($p < .05$) and between Communication Accuracy and Socially Oriented Trust ($p < .01$).

In hypothesis 7, Communication Frequency and Self-Interested Trust ($p < .05$) were positively and significantly related. There was also a significant positive relationship between Communication Frequency and Socially Oriented Trust ($p < .01$).

Finally, our control variable, Firm Size, was not significantly related to either Self-Interested Trust or Socially Oriented Trust.

## Conclusion

Overall, the results provide substantial support for the hypotheses offered in this study. Of the seven relationships proposed, four were fully supported, and two others received partial support.

As expected, we found that idiosyncratic training was positively related to higher levels of self-interested trust. Where training is tailored to a particular firm, it is likely that one party has invested significant resources to provide the training. Because it is in their best economic interest that the relationship continues, it might be anticipated that the firms investing these resources will make efforts to behave in a trustworthy manner. Contrary to expectations, the proposed relationship between idiosyncratic training and socially oriented trust was not significant. We had anticipated that as one party behaved in a trustworthy manner, even though the behavior was economically motivated, a foundation would be laid for higher levels of trust to evolve. This relationship was not observed.

Where substantial uncertainty existed in the design or delivery of training, we found that levels of both self-interested trust and socially oriented trust between firms and their suppliers were lower. These lower levels of trust likely resulted because of the greater potential for opportunistic behavior. Here, firms may have found that they had to direct their energies toward monitoring suppliers instead of building relationships.

The hypothesized relationship between vendor dependency and trust was partially supported. It was anticipated that where training managers perceived that their suppliers were dependent on them for business that higher levels of trust would be observed. Specifically, we believed that higher levels of trust would be reported because training vendors would make deliberate attempts to please their customers and that these positive actions might provide a basis for trust to emerge. While results demonstrated a significant relationship between vendor dependency and socially oriented trust, the expected relationship between vendor dependency and self-interested trust was not supported by the data. It is possible that respondents, at least in the short term, perceived seemingly altruistic actions as simply self-serving behaviors on the part of these vendors to protect their own interests and so were not inclined to believe that the training suppliers were actually demonstrating a commitment to the respondent firms.

Results also showed a positive relationship between contractual specificity and both self-interested and socially oriented trust. It is likely that more detailed contracts, where the responsibilities of each party and performance expectations were clearly defined, helped to mitigate the impact of opportunistic behaviors. This, in turn, was beneficial in both forming the basis for trusting relations and helping trust grow to higher levels.

We also found that where there was accurate and frequent communication between firms and their training suppliers, higher levels of trust emerged. Where respondents reported more accurate and frequent communication behaviors, it is likely that firms and training providers had a clearer understanding of each others' needs and capabilities and shared a sense of loyalty and responsibility for each other.

Finally, it should be noted that the expected relationship between a firm's outsourcing KSAs and trust was not supported. We anticipated that where a firm had experience in outsourcing, the potential for opportunistic behavior would be lower and trusting relations would emerge and evolve. However, a firm's experience level in dealing with outside suppliers was not significantly related to either self-interested trust or socially oriented trust. Although it is not entirely clear why this result was observed, it is possible that because of unfavorable experiences with previous outsourcing providers, training managers were more skeptical of external vendors and were reluctant to form trusting relations.

**Limitations of the Study.** Although this study represents an important first step in understanding aspects of the customer-vendor relationship where training is outsourced, it contains several limitations that should be addressed in future research. First, we collected data on the dependent and independent measures from the same key informant. The training manager is likely the individual best positioned to provide data on the variables in this study, but it is possible that a general response bias is affecting the results or that another person inside the firm might have had better information with which to respond to certain survey items. Future research might benefit from designs that avoid collecting all measures from the same key informant. For example, it may be possible to collect data from both the customer and the external training vendor.

Second, our sample was limited to ASTD members who had listed their job title as training manager or training director. Our concern was that by including additional job titles, we would survey individuals who would likely not have direct responsibility for the training function at their organization. However, by not selecting a random sample of individuals from the ASTD member listing, we have limited the extent to which the results can be generalized to other contexts.

Third, because this study was limited to firms that both had a training manager and were involved in outsourcing at least some of their training, it is possible that firms too small to employ training specialists were excluded. Thus, it may not be possible to generalize the findings in this research to these firms.

Fourth, our study asked respondents to comment on their training programs in general and did not focus on particular aspects of training. Future research that examines certain steps of the training process (for example, needs assessment or design of training) or focuses on particular types of training (for example, on-line or simulation) might prove beneficial.

Finally, these results are based on a cross-sectional survey. Thus, our ability to draw causal inferences is limited. Future research might well benefit from longitudinal designs that allow for causal inferences.

***Practical Implications.*** Firms increasingly rely on training vendors not only because of the cost savings often attributed to outsourcing, but also because of training suppliers' specialized expertise. However, firms must also realize that by entrusting their training needs to an outside party, they assume certain risks. For instance, training is often closely linked to a firm's ability to maintain a competitive advantage (Huselid et al., 1997; Wright & Snell, 1998). Thus, the practice of outsourcing training can potentially result in undesirable long-term consequences. For instance, where firms do not have amiable, trusting relations with their training vendors, these suppliers may be more inclined to engage in opportunistic behaviors that ultimately prove detrimental to the client (for example, revealing important aspects of an organization's training programs to other customers).

Unfortunately, the literature offers few guidelines to training managers on how best to establish, and then maintain, trusting relationships with their training vendors. This is problematic not only because of the reduced risk of opportunistic actions where trust exists, but also because previous interfirm research has established the important role of trust in generating additional positive outcomes (Child, 2001; Swan et al., 1988; Zaheer et al., 1998). Thus, this study represents an important first step in identifying factors that are significantly related to the levels of both self-interested trust and socially oriented trust between firms and their external training providers.

Based on our analysis and applicable theory, this study suggests that attempts to eliminate uncertainties related to the design and delivery of training programs are essential in increasing levels of self-interested trust. Results suggest that accurate and frequent communication between firms and their training suppliers is useful toward achieving this objective. However, complete and detailed contractual agreements were found to be a particularly important mechanism in mitigating these uncertainties.

In addition, results indicate that managers should not immediately disregard outsourcing when dealing with specialized training needs. This is not to suggest that training managers outsource training that may represent a sustainable competitive advantage for their firms. However, our findings indicate that where specialized training is outsourced, higher levels of self-interested trust are possible. In fact, where investments are made by a firm or a vendor to provide firm-specific training, the firm or vendor may engage in seemingly unselfish behaviors designed to ensure that the relationship continues.

Results also demonstrated significant levels of association between factors in this study and more evolved forms of socially oriented trust. As with self-interested trust, uncertainty with the design and delivery of training reduced levels of socially oriented trust. In addition, detailed contractual agreements helped to mitigate the impact of uncertainty. However, it was positive communication behaviors that were found to be most influential.

Specifically, we found that managers reporting more accurate and frequent exchanges with their training vendors also enjoyed higher levels of socially oriented trust. When firms and training vendors interact on a regular basis and are open in their exchanges regarding training issues, suppliers are able to use their resources in a way that ensures training programs are designed and delivered to best meet the needs of their clients. In time, client firms and suppliers come to understand each other better and develop a sense of loyalty and responsibility to each other.

In summary, this study offers important insights into how levels of trust are influenced by factors involved in outsourcing training activities to external providers. Specifically, the study suggests that certain factors are more important in establishing self-interested trust and that others might be crucial in helping trust evolve to more socially oriented forms.

# Appendix: Questionnaire Items and Factor Loadings

| Scale and Item | Factor | | | | | | | | |
|---|---|---|---|---|---|---|---|---|---|
| | 1 | 2 | 3 | 4 | 5 | 6 | 7 | 8 | 9 |
| **Self-Interested Trust** | | | | | | | | | |
| *Our outside training suppliers . . .* | | | | | | | | | |
| 1. have acted in self-serving ways. (R) | .43 | | | | | | | | |
| 2. have never taken advantage of us. | .64 | | | | | | | | |
| 3. have always looked after our best interests. | .66 | | | | | | | | |
| **Socially Oriented Trust** | | | | | | | | | |
| *Managers in our firm and our outside training suppliers . . .* | | | | | | | | | |
| 1. understand each others' behaviors well.[a] | | .61 | | | | | | | |
| 2. share a sense of loyalty to one another. | | .60 | | | | | | | |
| 3. feel a sense of responsibility to each other.[a] | | .59 | | | | | | | |
| **Idiosyncratic Training** | | | | | | | | | |
| *The training provided to us by outside suppliers . . .* | | | | | | | | | |
| 1. would have to be significantly changed if it were to be used in other contexts. | | | .62 | | | | | | |
| 2. is specifically designed to meet our needs.[b] | | | .62 | | | | | | |
| 3. is off-the-shelf training that could be used by many other businesses. (R) | | | .68 | | | | | | |
| **Program Uncertainty** | | | | | | | | | |
| *Our outside training suppliers . . .* | | | | | | | | | |
| 1. work in a way that is difficult for us to monitor. | | | | .45 | | | | | |
| 2. could be deceptive in their business dealings without us finding out. | | | | .88 | | | | | |
| 3. could take advantage of us without us knowing it. | | | | .86 | | | | | |
| **Vendor Dependency** | | | | | | | | | |
| *Our outside training suppliers . . .* | | | | | | | | | |
| 1. rely on our business to remain profitable.[a] | | | | | .80 | | | | |
| 2. depend on our business for continued success.[b] | | | | | .83 | | | | |
| 3. cannot afford to lose us as a customer. | | | | | .77 | | | | |
| 4. depend on us more than we do on them. | | | | | .68 | | | | |

*(Continued)*

# Appendix (Continued)

| Scale and Item | Factor | | | | | | | | |
|---|---|---|---|---|---|---|---|---|---|
| | 1 | 2 | 3 | 4 | 5 | 6 | 7 | 8 | 9 |
| **Outsourcing KSAs** *The managers here who work with outside training suppliers. . . .* | | | | | | | | | |
| 1. have worked with many different training suppliers. | | | | | | .70 | | | |
| 2. have a lot of experience dealing with vendors in the training area. | | | | | | .79 | | | |
| 3. are able to spend a lot of time monitoring these suppliers' performance. | | | | | | .77 | | | |
| 4. devote a great deal of time evaluating the performance of these suppliers. | | | | | | .68 | | | |
| **Contractual Specificity** *The agreements with our outside training suppliers. . . .* | | | | | | | | | |
| 1. are as complete as possible.[a] | | | | | | | .77 | | |
| 2. clearly outline the responsibilities of each party.[b] | | | | | | | .84 | | |
| 3. provide clear descriptions of required performance levels. [b] | | | | | | | .70 | | |
| 4. are specific and detailed.[b] | | | | | | | .74 | | |
| **Communication Accuracy** *Managers in our firm and our outside training suppliers. . . .* | | | | | | | | | |
| 1. trust that the information they receive from each other is correct.[c] | | | | | | | | .78 | |
| 2. feel confident that the information they exchange is reliable.[c] | | | | | | | | .76 | |
| **Communication Frequency** *Managers in our firm and our outside training suppliers. . . .* | | | | | | | | | |
| 1. talk to each other often. | | | | | | | | | .83 |
| 2. communicate frequently. | | | | | | | | | .85 |
| 3. exchange information in a timely manner.[c] | | | | | | | | | .65 |
| Eigenvalues | 1.67 | 1.48 | 1.52 | 1.91 | 2.57 | 2.38 | 2.81 | 1.62 | 2.33 |

*Note:* All items were measured on a five-point Likert-type scale where possible responses ranged from Strongly Disagree (1) to Strongly Agree (5). Factor loadings lower than .40 have been excluded from the table. R 5 reverse coded.

[a]Item based on Klaas, McClendon, and Gainey (2000).

[b]Item based on Nooteboom, Berger, and Noorderhaven (1997).

[c]Item based on Mohr and Spekman (1994).

# References

Adler, P. S. (2003). Making the HR outsourcing decision. *MIT Sloan Management Review, 45,* 53–60.

Anderson, E., Lodish, L. M., & Weitz, B. (1987). Resource allocation behavior in conventional channels. *Journal of Marketing Research, 24,* 254–262.

Anderson, E., & Weitz, B. (1989). Determinants of continuity in conventional industrial channel dyads. *Marketing Science, 8,* 310–323.

Aubert, B. A., Rivard, S., & Patry, M. (1996). A transaction cost approach to outsourcing behavior: Some empirical evidence. *Information and Management, 30,* 51–64.

Baker, D. (1996). Are you throwing money away by outsourcing? *Personnel Journal, 75,* 105–107.

Bassi, L. J., Cheney, S., & Van Buren, M. (1997, November). Training industry trends 1997. *Training and Development,* 46–59.

Borthick, S. (2001). Outsourcing trends: Customers and market mature. *Business Communications Review, 31,* 28–32.

Bradach, J. L., & Eccles, R. G. (1989). Markets versus hierarchies: From ideal types to plural forms. In W. R. Scott (Ed.), *Annual Review of Sociology* (pp. 97–118). Palo Alto, CA: Annual Reviews.

Child, J. (2001). Trust—The fundamental bond in global collaboration. *Organizational Dynamics, 29,* 274–288.

Daft, R., & Lengel, R. (1986). Organizational information requirements, media richness, and structural design. *Management Science, 32,* 554–571.

Dasgupta, P. (1988). Trust as a commodity. In D. Gambetta (Ed.), *Trust: Making and breaking cooperative relations* (pp. 49–72). Oxford: Basil Blackwell.

Devlin, G., & Bleackley, M. (1988). Strategic alliances—guidelines for success. *Long Range Planning, 21,* 18–23.

Greer, C. R., Youngblood, S. A., & Gray, D. A. (1999). Human resource management outsourcing: The make or buy decision. *Academy of Management Executive, 13,* 85–96.

Gulati, R. (1995). Does familiarity breed trust? The implications of repeated ties for contractual choice in alliances. *Academy of Management Journal, 38,* 85–112.

Harkins, P. J., Brown, S. M., & Sullivan, R. (1995). Shining new light on a growing trend. *HR Magazine, 40,* 75–79.

Huselid, M. A., Jackson, S. E., & Schuler, R. S. (1997). Technical and strategic human resource management effectiveness as determinants of firm performance. *Academy of Management Journal, 39,* 949–969.

Industry Report 2000: The money. (2000). *Training, 37,* 51–55.

Kaeter, M. (1995). An outsourcing primer. *Training and Development, 45,* 20–25.

Klaas, B. S., McClendon, J., & Gainey, T. W. (2000). Managing HR in the small and medium enterprise: The impact of professional employer organizations. *Entrepreneurship Theory and Practice, 25,* 107–124.

Kramer, R. M. (1993). Cooperation and organizational identification. In K. Murnighan (Ed.), *Social psychology in organizations: Advances in theory and research* (pp. 244–268). Upper Saddle River, NJ: Prentice Hall.

Kramer, R. M. (1996). Divergent realities and convergent disappointments in the hierarchic relation: Trust and the intuitive. In R. M. Kramer & T. R. Tyler (Eds.) *Trust in organizations: Frontiers of theory and research* (pp. 216–245). Thousand Oaks, CA: Sage.

Laabs, J. J. (1993). Successful outsourcing depends on critical factors. *Personnel Journal, 72,* 51–60.

Lepak, D. P., & Snell, S. A. (1998). Virtual HR: Strategic human resource management in the 21st century. *Human Resource Management Review, 8,* 215–234.

Lewicki, R. J., & Bunker, B. B. (1996). Developing and maintaining trust in work relationships. In R. M. Kramer & T. R. Tyler (Eds.), *Trust in organizations: Frontiers of theory and research* (pp. 114–139). Thousand Oaks, CA: Sage.

Logan, M. S. (2000). Using agency theory to design successful outsourcing relationships. *International Journal of Logistics Management, 11,* 21–32.

Luhmann, N. (1988). Familiarity, confidence, and trust: Problems and alternatives. In D. Bambetta (Ed.), *Trust: Making and breaking of cooperative relations* (pp. 94–107). Oxford: Blackwell.

Lyons, B., & Mehta, J. (1997). Contracts, opportunism, and trust: Self-interest and social orientation. *Cambridge Journal of Economics, 21,* 239–257.

McAllister, D. J. (1995). Affect- and cognition-based trust as foundations for interpersonal cooperation in organizations. *Academy of Management Journal, 38,* 24–59.

McCauley, D. P., & Kuhnert, K. W. (1992). A theoretical review and empirical investigation of employee trust in management. *Public Administration Quarterly, 16,* 265–283.

Mishra, A. K. (1996). Organizational responses to crises: The centrality of trust. In R. M. Kramer & T. R. Tyler (Eds.), *Trust in organizations: Frontiers of theory and research* (pp. 261–287). Thousand Oaks, CA: Sage.

Mohr, J., & Spekman, R. (1994). Characteristics of partnership success: Partnership attributes, communication behavior, and conflict resolution techniques. *Strategic Management Journal, 15* (February), 135–152.

Moore, K. R. (1998). Trust and relationship commitment in logistics alliances: A buyer perspective. *International Journal of Purchasing and Materials Management, 34,* 24–37.

Neter, J., Wasserman, W., & Kutner, M. (1990). *Applied linear statistical models.* Burr Ridge, IL: Irwin.

Niederkofler, M. (1991). The evolution of strategic alliances: Opportunities for managerial influence. *Journal of Business Venturing, 6,* 237–257.

Nooteboom, B. (1996). Trust, opportunism and governance: A process and control model. *Organizational Studies, 17,* 985–1010.

Nooteboom, B., Berger, H., & Noorderhaven, N. G. (1997). Effects of trust and governance on relational risk. *Academy of Management Journal, 40,* 308–338.

Ring, P. S., & Van de Ven, A. (1992). Structuring cooperative relationships between organizations. *Strategic Management Journal, 13,* 483–498.

Rousseau, D. M., Sitkin, S. B., Burt, R. S., & Camerer, C. (1998). Not so different after all: A cross-discipline view of trust. *Academy of Management Review, 23,* 393–404.

Shapiro, D. L., Sheppard, B. H., & Cheraskin, L. (1992, October). Business on a handshake. *Negotiation Journal,* 365–377.

Shelanski, H. A., & Klein, P. G. (1995). Empirical work in transaction cost economics. *Journal of Law, Economics, and Organization, 11,* 335–361.

Sheppard, B. H., & Tuchinsky, M. (1996). Micro-OB and the network organization. In R. M. Kramer & T. R. Tyler (Eds.), *Trust in organizations: Frontiers of theory and research* (pp. 140–165). Thousand Oaks, CA: Sage.

Swan, J. E., Trawick, I. F., Rink, D. R., & Roberts, J. J. (1988). Measuring dimensions of purchaser trust of industrial salespeople. *Journal of Personal Selling and Sales Management, 8,* 1–9.

Takeishi, A. (2001). Bridging inter- and intra-firm boundaries: Management of supplier involvement in automobile product development. *Strategic Management Journal, 22,* 403–433.

Webber, S. S. (2002). Leadership and trust facilitating cross-functional team success. *Journal of Management Development, 21,* 201–214.

Williamson, O. E. (1975). *Markets and hierarchies: Analysis and antitrust implications.* New York: Free Press.

Wright, P. M., & Snell, S. (1998). Toward a unifying framework for exploring fit and flexibility in strategic human resource management. *Academy of Management Review, 23,* 756–772.

Zaheer, A., McEvily, B., & Perrone, V. (1998). Does trust matter? Exploring the effects of interorganizational and interpersonal trust on performance. *Organizational Science, 9,* 141–159.

Zeffane, R. (1995). The widening scope of interorganizational networking: Economic, sectoral and social dimensions. *Leadership and Organization Development Journal, 16,* 26–33.

*Thomas W. Gainey is associate professor in the Department of Management, Richards College of Business, at the State University of West Georgia in Carrollton.*

*Brian S. Klaas is professor of management and chair of the Management Department at the Darla Moore School of Business at the University of South Carolina in Columbia.*

For bulk reprints of this article, please call (201) 748-8789.

# Invited Reaction: Outsourcing Relationships Between Firms and Their Training Providers: The Role of Trust

*Michael P. Leimbach*

*Outsourcing in the training and development industry has been steadily increasing and shows no indication of slowing (Sugrue & Kim, 2004). Gainey and Klaas's study shines light on the role of interfirm trust in effective outsourcing relationships. This reaction addresses a methodological question of the effect of the rating target on the results, but focuses on possible extensions of this research. Specific extensions include a deeper examination of factors contributing to Self Interested and Socially Oriented Trust, differentiating types of outsourcing relationships, and examining the perception of both the buyers and providers of outsourcing services.*

The role of outsourcing within the training and development function is expanding. Recent reports conclude that some segments of the learning outsourcing industry grew by 150 percent from 2002 to 2003 and may grow 400 percent over the next five years (Meister, 2004). This expansion makes it clear that there is a critical need to understand the characteristics that make for effective outsourcing. Gainey and Klaas have made an important start to this effort by exploring a vital element to successful outsourcing: interfirm trust. They have provided convincing evidence that a number of variables affect both self-interested and socially oriented trust and that critical components of this relation include the accuracy and frequency of communication and the specificity of contractual relationships.

The results of Gainey and Klaas's study shine light on the important topic of trust and raise important questions about the future direction for research on interfirm trust. I address the article from two perspectives. First, I address two questions about the article itself: one a methodological issue and the second a question on interpretation. I then turn to a discussion of some potential extensions of this topic with the hope that future research will provide a deeper understanding of how trust is created under different outsourcing conditions.

## Methodological Issue: The Target of Trust

In their research, Gainey and Klaas asked training managers and directors to rate their training suppliers as a whole. That is, the raters consider all of their training suppliers as a group and then rate their overall impressions. Although there are certain advantages to this approach, there is also a critical limitation: trust tends to be target specific (Giffin, 1967). Thus, a firm may trust one provider very highly and another one less so. Although there are some generalizations of trust to a class (for example, most children tend to trust police, and many adults tend not to trust politicians), trust is generally directed toward a specific person or firm.

By having firms rate training suppliers in general rather than specifically, Gainey and Klaas may have muted their results. As individual raters subconsciously average their opinions about a number of firms, the overall ratings regress to the mean. This possibility is supported by the measures of central tendency reported by Gainey and Klaas. The ratings on the nine dependent and independent variables were very close to the midpoint of their five-point Likert scale, ranging from 2.39 to 3.78. Also, the standard deviations were relatively small, indicating a somewhat leptokurtic distribution that is typical when ratings regress to the mean, or in this case, the midpoint in the scale.

This methodological approach could have one of two outcomes. This phenomenon could have caused the correlations to be lower than might have been observed if ratings had been more target specific. Alternatively, it could have led to spurious results, which is a possibility given that only 22 percent of the variance in Self-Interested Trust was accounted for in the regression analysis.

It would be valuable to replicate the study, but instead of asking for general supplier ratings have the firms rate the actions and perceptions of a single supplier or have them rate two suppliers separately—one for which they have a high level of satisfaction, the other a lower level of satisfaction. This should increase the variability of the ratings, flatten the distribution curve, and strengthen the regression coefficients. This expansion of Gainey and Klaas's methodology could also afford the opportunity to explore the relations between trust and firm satisfaction with the outsourcing service. Although a large amount of research shows a high correlation between trust in a salesperson and sales performance satisfaction (Churchill, Ford, Hartley, & Walker, 1985; Soldow & Thomas, 1984), little is known about this relation in the training outsourcing context specifically.

## Interpretation Issue: Differences in Predicting Types of Trust

One aspect of Gainey and Klaas's results I would have liked the authors to expand on was the difference in the regression coefficients between Self-Interested Trust and Socially Oriented Trust. Although it was not one of their original hypotheses, I was struck by how much better the variables were in predicting Socially Oriented Trust than Self-Interested Trust. Over twice as much variance in the Socially Oriented Trust scale was accounted for by the dependent variables than for Self-Interested Trust. Also, the factors contributing most to the regression coefficients were quite different. The overwhelming majority of the variance in Self-Interested Trust was accounted for by Contractual Specificity, while the two communication factors (Communication Accuracy and Communication Frequency) were by far the largest contributors to Socially Oriented Trust.

Although Gainey and Klaas's hypotheses all postulated that the same variables would contribute to both Self-Interest and Socially Oriented Trust, the results suggest that very different conditions tend to be the primary drivers of these types of trust. It would be interesting to explore these differences. The results also suggest that the conditions that create Self-Interested Trust at the beginning of a firm-supplier relationship may have a negligible effect on longer-term Socially Oriented trust. Thus, firm and supplier behavior needs to change over the course of a relationship if longer-term Socially Oriented Trust is to be developed. This would be especially interesting from a global perspective. In many cultures, particularly China and Japan, contract specificity can serve as a barrier to the development of trust (Wang, Brislin, Wang, Williams, & Chan, 2000).

It would be valuable to speculate on the kinds of factors that would predict one type of trust but not the other, or might have a negative contribution to one but a positive contribution to the other and to expand this research to a more global perspective.

## Trust and Levels of System Integration

The Gainey and Klaas study focused on understanding characteristics affecting different types of trust in an outsourcing relationship. The study did not differentiate levels of outsourcing as a factor. The authors defined outsourcing as any use of a vendor or supplier to provide training resources or training materials to a firm. Although this is an important prerequisite to this type of investigation, it led me to wonder about the impact of different types of outsourcing relationships and their potential impact on trust.

As we know, there are many forms of outsourcing relationships: purchasing training materials, hiring trainers, and leasing e-learning management systems, among others. One valuable way of differentiating types of outsourcing is by the degree of systems integration required of the two firms to deliver the training and development capability (Jackson, 1985). At one end of the continuum, firms purchase materials or hire a trainer to deliver learning content. At the other extreme, firms outsource the entire training and development management process. This latter form of outsourcing, business process outsourcing (BPO), is the fastest-growing segment of the outsourcing market (Meister, 2004; Think Equity Partners, 2003). When a firm uses BPO, it gains greater systems benefits from its relationships with suppliers, but at the price of increased switching costs for the firm (Jackson, 1985). Thus, there is a growing need to better understand how factors like trust bear on the success of these relationships because as a firm moves to higher levels of system integration, trust needs to strengthen in both directions.

Switching costs consist of those costs a purchasing firm experiences when it switches suppliers (Jackson, 1985). As a firm moves up the continuum of increased systems benefits, switching costs increase. For example, within the training and development industry, at the low end of the continuum a firm may contract with a supplier to deliver routine application software training. In this situation, there are minimal monetary costs associated with switching to another supplier; the materials and training easily substitute for one another. The primary switching costs are the intangibles—for example, the personal relations with the trainer and the supplier's knowledge of the firm's business.

At a slightly higher level, a company may purchase off-the-shelf leadership, sales, or customer service training. Switching costs increase somewhat because the training now embeds a point of view, specific terminology, or specific process in the organization. Switching to another provider means that either the employees trained by the new supplier will experience a different approach to sales process management, for example, or the firm will need to retrain salespeople to maintain a consistent approach to their market. These carry both monetary and intangible switching costs.

At a still higher level of systems integration, an organization does not just adopt a supplier's sales process training, but may incorporate work process forms, provide sales manager training, and configure the firm's sales force automation tool to support that sales process. These actions further integrate the learning into work performance, creating systems benefits for the firm, but they also result in much larger switching costs. Changing to another supplier would mean retraining managers and salespeople, reprogramming the sales force automation tool, and creating new process tools in addition to the other switching costs.

When a firm goes further and outsources the delivery and management of its entire training function, the switching costs could be exponentially larger. Most BPO relationships also involve the introduction of new information technologies: learning management systems, Web-based training programs, employee resource planning systems, and learning content management systems. While the introduction of these systems has been shown to reduce costs and improve learning outcomes (Greengard, 2004), switching to a new supplier could mean the entire reconstruction of business-critical databases and electronic-based learning delivery systems, and result in very great switching costs.

Clearly, the level of interfirm trust required is much higher as system benefits and switching costs go up. It could be valuable to both firms and suppliers to know the extent of that relationship and the factors that affect the relationship between system benefits and trust.

## The Supplier Perspective

Finally, in examining these results, I could not help but speculate on the views from the other side of the relationship: the supplier. Gainey and Klaas effectively examine the relationship between outsourcing and the buying firm's perception of trust. What would be equally useful would be an examination of this issue from the supplier's perspective.

There are a number of actions that suppliers take to build trust in their relationships with client firms. Previous research has shown that some supplier behaviors and characteristics are related to increased trust, such as perceived firm commonality, supplier competence, consistency, and clarity of intent (Churchill et al., 1985; Kudisch, 1989; Soldow & Thomas, 1984). Understanding the actions suppliers take to increase trust, the characteristics of the firm that influence the type of trust required, and the influence of system benefits and switching costs on the level of trust necessary for an effective relationship are all critical components to building a model of outsourcing effectiveness in the training and development industry.

## Conclusion

Gainey and Klaas have provided a good base for moving forward in the exploration of interfirm trust related to training outsourcing. In addition to the suggestions offered in their discussion, I believe that we could begin to build a more complete model of interfirm trust by differentiating the factors associated with self-interested and socially oriented trust and researching the impact of systems integration, cultural effects, and the actions suppliers take to strengthen trust. By understanding the conditions suitable to development of trust, we can help both firms and providers serve the learning and development needs of employees more effectively.

## References

Churchill, G. A., Ford, N. M., Hartley, S. W., & Walker, O. C. (1985). The determinants of salesperson performance: A meta-analysis. *Journal of Marketing Research, 22,* 103–118.

Giffin, K. (1967). The contribution of studies of source credibility to a theory of interpersonal trust in the communication process. *Psychological Bulletin, 68,* 104–120.

Greengard, S. (2004, July). Pulling the plug. *Workforce Management,* 43–46.

Jackson, B. (1985). *Winning and keeping industrial customers: The dynamics of customer relationships.* San Francisco: New Lexington Press.

Kudisch, J. D. (1989). *A factor analytic examination of managerial credibility.* Unpublished master's thesis, University of Central Florida.

Meister, J. C. (2004). How will interest in outsourcing change the CLO's role? *Chief Learning Officer, 3* (9), 62.

Soldow, G. F., & Thomas, G. P. (1984). Relational communication: Form versus content in the sales interaction. *Journal of Marketing, 48,* 84–93.

Sugrue, B., & Kim, K-H. (2004). *2004 State of the industry.* Alexandria, VA: American Society for Training and Development.

Think Equity Partners. (2003, May 29). *ASTD 2003: In search of the hockey stick.* San Francisco: Think Equity Partners.

Wang, M. M., Brislin, R. W., Wang, W., Williams, D., & Chan, J. H. (2000). *Turning bricks into jade: Critical incidents for mutual understanding among Chinese and Americans.* Yarmouth, ME: Intercultural Press.

*Michael P. Leimbach is vice president of research and design at Wilson Learning Worldwide in Edina, Minnesota.*

# The Growth of Supply and Demand of Occupational-Based Training and Certification in the United States, 1990–2003

*Shani D. Carter*

*The 1990s and early 2000s saw the increased development of advanced training, skills standards, and certification exams by private organizations in the United States. Employers began accepting these skill certifications in lieu of traditional on-the-job training, thereby encouraging employees to acquire more credentials. This article examines the increase in the number of skill certifications available, discusses legislative causes of these increases, and notes the current lack of published peer-reviewed analyses of statistical reliability and validity of certification exams. It presents a call for future research to determine the usefulness of certification.*

During the 1990s, the industrial shift away from manufacturing and toward service in the United States, especially the expansion of the software and hardware fields, led employers to increase demand for highly skilled employees. Concurrently, private organizations rapidly increased the number and types of skill certifications available. These certifications are skill based (rather than theory based) and generally take less than one year to complete. Although there seems to have been an exponential growth in the number of certifications available and in the number of people certified, there has been no systematic tracking of these increases (Silverberg, Warner, Goodwin, & Fong, 2002).

If employers are relying more on certification, then they may decrease their number of in-house training and development employees while certification organizations increase their number of trainers. The increase in certification would not, however, eliminate an organization's need for in-house trainers; rather, it changes their focus. The classic model of training defined four outcomes: reaction, learning, behavior, and results (Kirkpatrick, 1998). Trainers must become performance consultants (Dilworth, 2001) and begin to segue away from a focus on learning to a focus on behavior—how to teach trainees to transfer learning from certification to the job. Training and development professionals can evaluate their training programs to ensure transfer occurs and the organization receives sufficient return on investment (Garvaglia, 1993).

This article presents a review of the literature on certification exams, covering labor supply and demand, legislation, and types of certifications available. The model used is a time-series, supply-demand model (Cook & Campbell, 1979; Ehrenberg & Smith, 2000). Specifically, I examine whether the increased demand for skilled employees combined with the federal government's increased encouragement of certification programs led to an increase in the supply of certifications offered by private sector firms. I focus on programs outside the mainstream high school and college systems in order to demonstrate the private sector, entrepreneurial response of training and development organizations to the increased demand for skilled employees. Past research has shown that school-based training alone is insufficient to increase employee skills to the level required by employers (Bishop, 1993). I then present quantitative data examining whether the increased demand for skills was followed by an increase in supply of certifications offered. Finally, I present a call for future research on the extent of certification and the validity of certification exams.

## Theoretical Frame

The following discussion places vocational certification in the context of the larger educational system in the United States and covers the impact of legislation and increased employer demand for skilled employees.

*The Educational System in the United States.* In the United States, the educational system historically has been divided into three levels as defined by the federal government: grade school (kindergarten though grade 8), high school (college preparatory or vocational, grades 9 through 12), and college. Prior to 1990, high school graduates who were uninterested in attending college could gain useful skills by obtaining training from a private training organization or by attending training or apprenticeship programs with their employer or union. Aside from the apprenticeship and certification programs required by law (such as electrical or plumbing), these programs tended not to be standardized from site to site and were therefore not promoted, regulated, or tracked by the U.S. Department of Education or U.S. Department of Labor. In the 1990s, however, these programs began to be promoted by the federal government and employers as a means to ensure the availability of skilled labor to address the changes in the industrial mix and the growth of international competitiveness.

*Effect of Legislation on Supply of Advanced Training.* During the 1990s, the federal government passed legislation promoting vocational certification. This legislation created the National Skills Standards Board, which assisted private organizations in the development of skills standards and certifications.

*Certification-Related Legislation During the 1990s.* On April 18, 1991, President George H. W. Bush presented an education strategy, titled America 2000, to the public (U.S. Congress, 1991). This strategy was debated and refined during the 103rd and 104th Congresses and was presented for signature to President Bill Clinton as Goals 2000: Educate America Act on March 28, 1994 (U.S. Congress, 1992, 1994c). This act called for improvements at all levels of the educational system in the United States, including the adoption of nationally standardized bodies of knowledge. Specifically, the act was designed "to improve learning and teaching by providing a national framework for education reform; . . . [and] to promote the development and adoption of a voluntary national system of skill standards and certifications" (U.S. Congress, 1994c, p. H2215).

Congress strongly believed that improving skills standards was necessary to meet the challenges of advances in technology, industrial shifts, and increased competition in the global economy (U.S. Congress, 1994b). Secretary of Education Richard W. Riley and Secretary of Labor Robert B. Reich each appeared before congressional committees to discuss the need for high-quality training programs for people who do not enroll in a four-year college or university. Their goal was to work with the states, school districts, and employers to create education that would be "well-grounded in academics but also in the broad occupational areas that are relevant to real job needs" (Young, 1993, p. 7).

*Creation of the National Skills Standards Board.* One of the initiatives of Goals 2000 was the establishment of a quasi–private sector organization that would focus on skills certification standards. In designing the goals of the National Skills Standards Board (NSSB), Congress addressed three concerns: (1) employees' skills in the United States should meet or exceed the skills of employees in other countries, (2) educational institutions in the United States are fiercely protective of their autonomy, and (3) new standards should not conflict with or weaken existing standards. The legislation therefore stated that the NSSB should "ensure that skill standards meet or exceed the highest applicable standards used in other countries . . . [and] also the highest applicable standards used in the United States, including the apprenticeship standards registered under the National Apprenticeship Act. . . . The standards . . . are not [to be] used to undercut or dilute any existing standards" (U.S. Congress, 1994a, p. S1146).

The NSSB therefore was to use voluntary partnerships between business, labor, and education to develop skill standards systems, including training and testing (U.S. Congress, 1994b). Congress hoped that employees, employers, and educators would be enthusiastic regarding development of the standards. To date, the NSSB has supported development of skills standards and certifications for fifteen distinct industries, ranging from agriculture to utilities (NSSB, 2002a, 2003).

*Scope of Certification Topics.* Many private organizations, besides those affiliated with the NSSB, also developed numerous training programs and certification exams that measure a vast array of skills necessary in occupations such as secretary, auto mechanic, airline mechanic, computer programmer, compensation specialist, and physician, among many others. The educational levels required to enroll in these training programs range from high school education to doctoral education. Thus, it is possible for people of all ability levels to obtain advanced training and document some level of expertise in a given field. This wide availability of certification topics is especially important for employees who do not attend college, because they can use certification as a means of entry into challenging careers, thereby increasing their standard of living (Eck, 1993).

**Demand for Employees.** As the U.S. economy continued to move away from manufacturing and toward service, employers demanded more highly skilled employees and began to accept certifications as indicative of employee skills.

*Employer Demand for Employees with Advanced Training.* In the United States, employer demand for highly trained employees continues to increase (Pierce, 2000). This demand is driven by service sector firms, such as banking and software, that have high percentages of managerial, professional, and technical employees who must be highly skilled, flexible, and adaptable if the firms are to remain globally competitive (Bishop, 1996; Silvestri, 1997; U.S. Department of Labor, 1998, 2002). These advanced sectors of the economy continue to expand faster than sectors that historically have required employees to use less judgment and critical thinking, such as traditional manufacturing firms (Katz, Hwang, & Resnick, 1997). Furthermore, because the industrial mix and technology are changing rapidly, firms also require employees to have the ability to learn, so that employees can obtain new skills necessary to perform effectively in the changing environment (Thurow, 1997).

*Growth of Employer Acceptance of Certification.* Following the passage of Goals 2000, skills training and certification began to gain wider acceptance by employers (Hight, 1998). That is, employers began to rely more on outside training and development organizations instead of increasing the number of in-house trainers on their staffs. Unless an employer needs to train hundreds of employees each year, it is more cost-effective for the employer to send employees to outside training in specialized skills as needed than it is to hire a set of permanent in-house trainers for a series of topics. For example, advances in computer technology have led to a skills shortage, and "employers are increasingly embracing vocational certification, which is also becoming the norm in other industries" (Bellinger, 1996, p. 76). Employers use certified employees to fill positions such as systems and software engineers, systems analysts, programmers, repair technicians, and help desk staffers. This increased use of certification in the computer field is exactly the sort of outcome Congress desired when it ratified Goals 2000. Other areas of employment growth for employees with certification include human resources, repairers, technicians, welders, carpenters, electricians, and truck drivers (Krenek, 2000; Veum, 1993).

The growth in certification could help increase diversity in the labor force. This would occur because whites are more likely to receive on-the-job training than are blacks and Hispanics, but blacks and Hispanics are more likely to receive training from business schools and vocational or technical institutes (Veum, 1993). If blacks and Hispanics continue to receive vocational certification at the same relatively high rate and employer acceptance of vocational certification continues, then labor force outcomes for blacks and Hispanics will be better than they would otherwise be if employer demand for vocational certification did not increase.

**Supply of Employees.** In response to the increased employer demand for high skills, employees have begun to obtain higher skills as a means of entry to high-paying occupations.

*Supply of Employees with Advanced Training.* The increased demand for highly skilled employees has induced increases in the supply of skilled employees. For example, U.S. governors implemented initiatives to increase the high school graduation rate, which currently stands near 90 percent (Kaufman, Kwon, Klein, & Chapman, 1999; Snyder & Hoffman, 2003). Furthermore, the percentage of twenty-five to thirty-four year olds who have a college degree increased from 24 to 29 percent during the 1990s (this percentage had remained at 24 percent throughout the 1980s). In contrast, the percentage of twenty-five to thirty-four year olds with only a high school diploma remained at about 60 percent for the twenty-year period (U.S. Department of Commerce, 2000). These high school graduates who were uninterested in (or unqualified for) college began to seek certification as an alternative route to higher-paying jobs because employer demand for unskilled workers was shrinking and demand for skilled employees continued to exceed the supply. That is, employees will attend training if they expect it will have a positive impact on their later earnings (Lauer, 2002). This increasing shortage of skilled employees is demonstrated by the increasing wage differentials between college graduates and high school graduates during the 1980s and 1990s (Bishop, 1996; Bishop & Carter, 1991). For example, from 1996 to 2000, median annual earnings for high school graduates increased 26 percent (from $20,650 to $25,993) while median annual earnings for bachelor's degree holders increased 36 percent (from $35,672 to $48,440; Hecker, 2001; Silvestri, 1997).

*Methods for Employees to Obtain Advanced Training.* In order to achieve the higher skill levels required today, employees can earn college degrees or can acquire the skills through other means, such as training, independent study, continuing education, or job experience. Whichever route to skill acquisition is chosen, employees need a credential to indicate their skill levels to employers (Adelman, 2000). Some employees use a college degree as the credential, and employers can gauge the skill level of a college graduate based on the graduate's grade point average (GPA) and the rigor of the college that granted the degree.

Employees without a college degree (60 percent of high school graduates) can obtain training and use a skill certification as the credential. The training and skill certification can be provided by a private training organization, a certification-testing organization, a vocational school, or a college, (Veum, 1993). Prior to the mid-1990s, however, skill certification (besides that in vocational schools and colleges) was used in a limited number of fields, was rarely discussed in federal publications, and was deemed to be outside the mainstream educational system (Krenek, 2000).

## Hypothesis

The 1990s saw increased demand for highly skilled employees due to continued advances in technology and shifts in employment from manufacturing to services and high-tech industries. Concurrently, there was a growing shortage of highly skilled employees because 60 percent of high school graduates do not earn a college degree. The passage of Goals 2000 encouraged private organizations to address the gap between the supply and demand of skilled employees by developing standardized training, and the act also encouraged employers to accept skill certifications. Therefore, I hypothesize the following:

HYPOTHESIS 1. *There has been an increase in the number of fields for which private sector certification is offered that mirrors increases in demand for skilled employees in these fields.*

## Method

This article uses a time-series, supply-demand model. Specifically, I gathered time-series data on projected employment demand in fields that use certification and data on the number of certifications supplied in these fields.

***Employer Demand for Employees with Advanced Training and Certification.*** I gathered data from federal publications regarding the level of demand for employees with advanced training and certification and found that for the past twenty years, economists of the U.S. Department of Labor, Bureau of Labor Statistics (BLS) have published biannual projections of occupational employment in the *Monthly Labor Review.* These projections estimate employment growth in detailed occupations for the following ten years. The projections are based on assumptions regarding population growth, consumer demand, economic growth, international trade, technology, employer demand for skills, and educational achievement of employees. I used the employment projections as a gauge of future demand for highly trained employees because the projections are based partially on educational achievement.

There are limitations to using these data, however. Prior to the projections published in 1997, neither the BLS, the Bureau of the Census, nor the

Department of Education gathered data on technical training or vocational education except for that which led to a high school diploma or college degree. The BLS wrote that "schooling in other than regular schools is counted only if the credits obtained are regarded as transferable to a school in the regular school system" (U.S. Department of Labor and U.S. Department of Commerce, 1996, p. 8).

Therefore, prior to the mid-1990s, the extent of technical training and vocational education in the United States was relatively hidden from educators, researchers, employers, and job seekers. For example, the BLS employment projections published during and before November 1993 reported educational attainment as (1) less than twelve years, (2) high school graduate, (3) some college, and (4) college graduate (Fellerton, 1989; Silvestri & Lukasiewicz, 1991; Silvestri, 1993). Employment projections published in November 1995 contained no data regarding educational attainment (Silvestri, 1995).

From 1997 onward, the employment projections contained a larger number of categories of education, training, or work experience required and linked each occupation with one of the categories (Herman, 1999; Wash, 1995–1996). The eleven categories of educational attainment were (1) first professional degree; (2) doctoral degree; (3) master's degree; (4) work experience, plus a bachelor's or higher degree; (5) bachelor's degree; (6) associate degree; (7) postsecondary vocational training; (8) work experience in a related occupation; (9) long-term on-the-job training; (10) moderate-term on-the-job training; and (11) short-term on-the-job training (Silvestri, 1997; Braddock, 1999).

I focused on the employment projections for the postsecondary vocational training category to estimate the increased demand for advanced training and certification of employees without a college degree. The recent emphasis by the BLS on increased differentiation between levels of educational achievement may have been due to the passage of Goals 2000. With the increased demand for skilled employees during the 1990s came the realization that accurate employment projections could be made only if these employees were identified as a distinct group.

***Supply of Advanced Training and Certification.*** I gathered data from private, noncollegiate certification organizations at two points in time to determine the rate of growth of the number of certifications available. The goal was to ascertain the extent of training and certification available to the 60 percent of high school graduates who do not earn a college degree. The certifications I examined are those that are voluntary (not legally required for entry into a field) because I wished to focus on the private sector, entrepreneurial response of training and development organizations to the increased demand for skilled employees. I began my search with the literature from the Department of Education, the Department of Labor, the NSSB, and academic and practitioner journals. My goal at this stage was to determine the names of organizations offering certifications and the topics of these certifications.

Next, I conducted an Internet-based search for Web sites of the private organizations I had identified, which yielded information regarding the number and types of certifications available in 2000 and 2003. I also conducted an Internet-based search with search engines using terms such as *vocational training, vocational certification,* and *skill certification.* I limited the sample of organizations to those with an Internet presence because I believed the Internet to be the medium that could provide the broadest and most consistent data for all potential trainees and employers across the United States. Using data available only at a local unemployment office would have yielded data skewed toward that local area, and using data available only at a university library would have yielded data unavailable to the average employee or employer. Thus, I attempted to capture the data that would be available to the members of the U.S. labor market as a whole.

In 2000, I found 219 certifications offered in four major occupational areas (computer, health, management, and mechanic) by forty-seven private organizations. In 2003, I revisited these forty-seven organizations' Web sites to determine whether they had changed the number of certifications they offered.

At each Web site, I gathered the names and descriptions of certifications offered. If a certification name but not the description was changed between 2000 and 2003, this was counted as the same certification. If a certification name remained the same but the description was changed slightly to update it, this too was counted as the same certification. If one certification offered in 2000 was split into two certifications in 2003, these were counted as one certification in 2000 and two certifications in 2003, and vice versa if two certifications from 2000 were combined into one in 2003. In sum, I focused primarily on the descriptions of the certifications in gathering data.

I did not gather data on certifications that were legally required for entry into a field; specific to a single employer; or offered only by a college, university, or high school (although certifications were counted if they were offered by a noncollegiate private organization and offered at many sites, including some colleges). Thus, the sample consisted of certifications that could be obtained by an average high school graduate pursuing a high-skill job such as database manager. These certifications, which generally take less than one year to obtain, can significantly improve the labor market prospects of high school graduates in a relatively short time. Most of the certifications in the sample can be classified into one of four fields: computer related, mechanic, health and fitness, and human resources.

## Results

The results show that both employer demand for skilled employees and the number of certifications offered by private firms increased.

*Employer Demand for Employees with Advanced Training and Certification.* Federal projections indicated that employers would demand increasing numbers of employees with advanced skills across occupations requiring vocational education and for the four occupational groups in this study.

*All Occupations.* Federal data published regarding the number of jobs requiring vocational education indicates an increasing rate of growth in the number of these jobs. For example, the BLS estimated that the number of these jobs would grow by 7 percent during 1996–2006 and by the much faster rates of 14 percent during 1998–2008 and 18 percent during 2000–2010 (Table 1). This rate exceeds the projected growth rate of 15 percent for all occupations between 2000 and 2010. In addition to the fast rate of growth of these occupations, the number of job openings that require vocational training is significant. The BLS estimated that there will be 643,000 new jobs for employees with vocational training during 1998–2008 and 1.2 million new jobs during 2000–2010 (Table 1). Furthermore, these jobs will account for an increasing share of total job growth, rising from 3.2 percent for 1998–2008 to 5.5 percent for 2000–2010.

*Specific Occupations.* I also examined projected job growth by occupation for 1996–2010 for the four primary fields in our sample (computer, mechanic, health, and human resources). These data are shown in Table 2. I wanted to determine whether employment in these fields was projected to grow more rapidly than total employment was projected to grow, which I would expect to lead to an increase in the number of certifications offered in these fields, so that employees could gain the skills necessary to obtain these jobs.

The BLS estimated that between 1996–2006 and between 1998–2008, the growth rate of total employment would be 14 percent per decade (Table 2). This rate was projected to increase to 15 percent for 2000–2010. For computer-related jobs, the growth rate was much higher than the growth rate of total employment (58 percent for 1996–2006, 68 percent for 1998–2008, and 63 percent for 2000–2010). For mechanic jobs, the growth rate was slightly lower than the growth rate of total employment (13 percent for 1996–2006, 12 percent for 1998–2008, and 11 percent for 2000–2010). For health and nutrition jobs, the growth rate was similar to the growth rate of total employment (14 percent for 1996–2006, 12 percent for 1998–2008, and 15 percent for 2000–2010). For human resource jobs, the growth rate was slightly higher than the growth rate for total employment (14 percent for 1996–2006, 12 percent for 1998–2008, and 15 percent for 2000–2010). Thus, the growth rate of employment for occupations using certification exceeded the growth rate of total U.S. employment.

From these employment projections, we can determine whether the growth in number of certifications available mirrored the projected growth in employment demand. We would expect a very high growth rate in the number of computer certifications, moderate growth in the number of human resources and health certifications, and slight growth in the number of mechanic and health certifications.

# Table 1. Projected Employment Changes for Education and Training Categories, 1996–2010

| Education and Training Category | Employment (000s) 2000[a] | Growth (000s) | | | Growth (percent) | | | Percentage of Total Growth | | |
|---|---|---|---|---|---|---|---|---|---|---|
| | | 1996–2006 | 1998–2008 | 2000–2010 | 1996–2006 | 1998–2008 | 2000–2010 | 1996–2006 | 1998–2008 | 2000–2010 |
| Total, all occupations | 145,594 | 18,574 | 20,281 | 22,160 | 14 | 14 | 15 | 100.0 | 100.0 | 100.0 |
| Postsecondary vocational training | 6,678 | 598 | 643 | 1,213 | 7 | 14 | 18 | 4.6 | 3.2 | 5.5 |
| Work experience in related job | 10,456 | 1,211 | 1,316 | 1,102 | 12 | 12 | 11 | 6.5 | 6.5 | 5.0 |
| Short-term on-the-job training | 53,198 | 6,937 | 7,576 | 7,673 | 13 | 14 | 14 | 42.4 | 37.4 | 34.6 |
| Moderate-term on-the-job training | 27,671 | 1,468 | 1,430 | 3,123 | 9 | 7 | 11 | 11.1 | 7.1 | 14.1 |
| Long-term on-the-job training | 12,435 | 1,125 | 1,168 | 938 | 9 | 9 | 8 | 7.9 | 5.8 | 4.2 |
| Associate degree | 5,083 | 915 | 1,537 | 1,626 | 22 | 31 | 32 | 3.2 | 7.6 | 7.3 |
| Bachelor's degree | 17,801 | 4,017 | 4,217 | 4,006 | 25 | 24 | 23 | 14.5 | 20.8 | 18.1 |
| Bachelor's degree and work experience | 7,319 | 1,597 | 1,680 | 1,422 | 18 | 18 | 19 | 6.9 | 8.3 | 6.4 |
| Master's degree | 1,426 | 206 | 174 | 333 | 15 | 19 | 23 | 0.9 | 0.9 | 1.5 |
| First professional degree | 2,034 | 308 | 308 | 370 | 18 | 16 | 18 | 1.2 | 1.5 | 1.7 |
| Doctoral degree | 1,492 | 193 | 232 | 353 | 19 | 23 | 24 | 0.9 | 1.1 | 1.6 |

[a]Most recently available data.

Sources: Braddock (1999), Hecker (2001), Herman (1999), and Silvestri (1997).

**Table 2. Projected Employment Growth, Number of Organizations Offering Certification, and Number of Certifications Available**

| Field of Study | Percentage Projected Employment Growth[b] | | | Organizations | | | Certifications | | |
|---|---|---|---|---|---|---|---|---|---|
| | 1996–2006 | 1998–2008 | 2000–2010 | 2000 | 2003 | Change Percentage | 2000 | 2003 | Change Percentage |
| Total all certifications (occupations) | 14 | 14 | 15 | 47 | 65 | 38 | 219 | 584 | 165 |
| Total privately sponsored[a] | — | — | — | 47 | 38 | −19 | 219 | 416 | 90 |
| Computer hardware and software | 58 | 68 | 63 | 9 | 6 | −33 | 64 | 212 | 231 |
| Mechanic and laborer | 13 | 12 | 11 | 16 | 13 | −19 | 44 | 65 | 48 |
| Health, nutrition, and fitness | 14 | 12 | 15 | 5 | 3 | −40 | 21 | 20 | −5 |
| Management and human resources | 18 | 18 | 18 | 12 | 11 | −8 | 59 | 86 | 46 |
| Miscellaneous | — | — | — | 5 | 5 | 0 | 31 | 33 | 6 |
| Sponsored by NSSB or Department of Labor | — | — | — | 0 | 27 | — | 0 | 168 | — |

[a]Excluding those sponsored by the NSSB and the Department of Labor.

[b]Derived from Hecker (2001), Braddock (1999), and Silvestri (1997).

*Supply of Advanced Training and Certification.* Across occupations, the number of certifications offered by private firms increased. The rate of increase in specific occupations mirrored the rate of increase in employer demand of skilled employees.

*All Occupations.* In 2000, the forty-seven private organizations in the sample offered 219 certifications in four major occupational areas (computer, health, human resources, and mechanic; Table 2). By 2003, nine of these organizations ceased to exist or had merged with other organizations, indicating that the field of certification is not stagnant. Indeed, the thirty-eight remaining organizations had increased the number of certifications offered to 416, an increase of 90 percent (Table 2). Therefore, despite consolidation in the number of private firms, there was expansion in the number of certifications offered. Furthermore, twenty-seven additional organizations had developed 168 certifications under the auspices of the NSSB or the Department of Labor.

*Specific Occupations.* For the thirty-eight private organizations remaining in the sample in 2003, between the years 2000 and 2003, the number of computer-related certifications available increased by 231 percent (Table 2). Other fields for which certification has become important include mechanics, repairers, technicians, machinists, welders, carpenters, electricians, and truck drivers, for which the number of certifications available increased by 48 percent. In the human resource and management fields, the number of certifications available increased by 46 percent. Surprisingly, the number of certifications available in the health and fitness-related fields declined by 5 percent. This retrenchment was caused by an initial burst of overspecialization in clinical, health, and fitness certifications that was later found to be unnecessary (Table 3). Many of the highly specialized certifications were combined into broader topics.

*Specific Organizations.* Table 3 presents detail on the growth in specific certification topics. More than half (twenty of thirty-eight) of the organizations in the sample increased the number of certifications offered, while about one-third (fourteen of thirty-eight) maintained the number of certifications offered, and the remaining 10 percent (four of thirty-eight) decreased the number of certifications offered.

In the computer field, five of the six organizations increased the number of certifications offered. One organization decreased the number of certifications offered. In the mechanic field, seven of the thirteen organizations increased the number of certifications offered, while the remaining six organizations maintained the number of certifications offered. In the health-related field, one organization increased its number of certifications offered, one organization decreased its number offered, and one maintained its number offered. In the human resource and management field, five of the eleven organizations increased the number of certifications offered, one decreased the number offered, and the remaining five maintained the number offered.

## Table 3. General Subject Areas of Available Certifications

| Subject of Certification | Number of Tests, 2000 | Number of Tests, 2003 | Percentage Change | Internet Address |
|---|---|---|---|---|
| Computer hardware and software | | | | |
| Cisco | 10 | 41 | 310 | www.cisco.com |
| IBM Professional Certification Program | 19 | 120 | 532 | www.ibm.com |
| Oracle | 9 | 7 | −22 | www.education.oracle.com |
| Microsoft | 6 | 10 | 67 | www.microsoft.com |
| Telecommunications, computer, art, entertainment | 4 | 6 | 50 | www.scte.org |
| Other software and hardware | 16 | 28 | 75 | www.trainingplanet.com |
| Total computer | 64 | 212 | 231 | |
| Mechanic and laborer | | | | |
| Aircraft mechanic | 2 | 3 | 50 | www.nemac.com |
| Automobile and light truck repair | 6 | 9 | 50 | www.uticorp.com |
| Automotive Service Excellence | 11 | 17 | 55 | www.asecert.org |
| Auto glass technician | 2 | 6 | 200 | www.glass.org |
| Crane operators | 4 | 4 | 0 | www.nccco.org |
| Heat, ventilation, air conditioning, and refrigeration | 5 | 10 | 100 | www.natex.org |
| Mining | 1 | 1 | 0 | www.landman.org |
| Outdoor power equipment technician | 1 | 1 | 0 | www.eetc.org |
| Plastics technologist | 1 | 1 | 0 | www.4spe.org |
| Small engine repair | 5 | 6 | 20 | www.engineservice.com |
| Surveying | 2 | 2 | 0 | www.survmap.org |
| Safety supervisors | 1 | 2 | 100 | www.bcsp.com |
| Welder | 3 | 3 | 0 | www.welding.org |
| Total mechanic and laborer | 44 | 65 | 48 | |
| Health, nutrition, and fitness | | | | |
| Clinical health and fitness | 9 | 4 | −56 | www.acsm.org |
| Food preparation and serving | 9 | 13 | 44 | www.acfchefs.org |
| In-line skating instructor | 3 | 3 | 0 | www.iisa.org |
| Total health, nutrition, and fitness | 21 | 20 | −5 | |
| Management and human resources | | | | |
| Business, administration, and financial services | 3 | 3 | 0 | www.nacm.org |
| Certified Payroll Professional | 2 | 2 | 0 | www.americanpayroll.org |
| Employee benefits | 22 | 26 | 18 | www.ifebp.org |
| Employee compensation | 12 | 25 | 108 | www.acaonline.org |
| Education and training | 1 | 0 | −100 | www.chauncey.com |
| Finance and insurance | 3 | 3 | 0 | www.nacm.org |
| Human resources | 2 | 2 | 0 | www.shrm.org |
| International human resources | 2 | 3 | 50 | www.ipma-hr.org |
| Management | 4 | 13 | 225 | www.amanet.org |
| Office and administrative support: Legal | 2 | 3 | 50 | www.nals.org, ww.nala.org |
| Training and development | 6 | 6 | 0 | www.astd.org |
| Total human resources and management | 59 | 86 | 46 | |

*(Continued)*

Table 3.  General Subject Areas of Available Certifications (*Continued*)

| Subject of Certification | Number of Tests, 2000 | Number of Tests, 2003 | Percentage Change | Internet Address |
|---|---|---|---|---|
| Miscellaneous | | | | |
| Ergonomics | 1 | 3 | 200 | www.bcpe.org |
| Hospitality and tourism | 25 | 21 | −16 | www.ei-ahma.org |
| Meteorology | 2 | 2 | 0 | www.imageplaza.com |
| Substance abuse | 2 | 6 | 200 | www.ccb-inc.org |
| Retail, wholesale, real estate, and personal services | 1 | 1 | 0 | www.ssvolpart.org |
| Total miscellaneous | 31 | 33 | 6 | |
| Sponsored by NSSB or Department of Labor | | | | |
| Agriculture, forestry, fishing | 0 | 6 | — | www.irrigation.org |
| Building and grounds cleaning and maintenance | 0 | 31 | — | www.iicrc.org; natmi.org; pgms.org; gocampingamerica.com; bomi-edu.org; naahq.org; nchm.org; cm-instituteonline.com |
| Construction | 0 | 9 | — | www.csda.org; bcsp.org; www.aci-int.org |
| Electronics, fiber optics | 0 | 25 | — | www.eta-sda.com |
| Industrial quality, safety, maintenance | 0 | 34 | — | www.sme.org; asq.org; ifps.org; isa.org; nait.org; nasm.com; iscetstore.org |
| Lab and animal science | 0 | 7 | — | www.aalas.org; abka.com |
| Manufacturing | 0 | 34 | — | www.msscusa.org |
| Transport and material moving, logistics | 0 | 3 | — | www.iopp.org |
| Utilities, environmental and waste management | 0 | 19 | — | www.neha.org; beac.org; nrep.org |
| Total sponsored | 0 | 168 | — | |
| Total all certifications | 219 | 584 | 165 | |

## Discussion

Across occupations, there has been an increase in the number of certifications offered. This increase will have an impact on the practice of training and development for in-house trainers.

*Supply and Demand for Advanced Skills and Certification.* The overall trend is for growth in the field of certification, which was seemingly driven by increased demand for employees with specific skill sets. For example, the overall number of jobs for employees with postsecondary vocational education was projected to increase at an accelerating rate from 1996 to 2010 (7 percent from 1996–2006, 14 percent from 1998–2008, and 18 percent from 2000–2010). During the middle of this period (2000–2003), the number of certifications available by the organizations in the sample increased by 90 percent. If we include the certifications developed under the auspices of the NSSB and Department of Labor during 2000–2003, then the rate of growth in available certifications was 165 percent.

Examining demand for employees and supply of certifications by specific occupations shows that the increase in the number of certifications paralleled the increase in employer demand. For example, for computer-related jobs, the mean projected rate of growth for the 1996–2006, 1998–2008, and 2000–2010 periods (63 percent) far outpaced the projected rate of growth for all jobs (14 percent), just as the actual increase in the number of certifications offered from 2000 to 2003 (231 percent) far outpaced the rate of growth for all certifications (90 percent).

The other major occupations in the sample also saw projected job growth, and all but one saw increases in the number of certifications available. The mechanic and laborer occupations were projected to grow at a mean rate of 12 percent and saw an actual increase in certifications of 48 percent. The management and human resource occupations were projected to grow at a mean rate of 18 percent and saw an actual increase in the number of certifications of 46 percent. Conversely, the health, nutrition, and fitness occupations were projected to grow at a mean rate of 14 percent but saw a 5 percent decline in the number of certifications available. This converse result was due to initial overspecialization and later consolidation in certifications. It also could be due to the small sample size, because there were only three firms and twenty certifications offered in the sample in 2003.

The field of certification has grown so large (and presumably lucrative) that publishers (such as Learning Express) had begun offering test preparation for the exams similar to the test preparation offered for the Scholastic Aptitude Test (SAT; Charters, 1999). Furthermore, since September 1999, MediaTec has published *Certification Magazine* and study guides as resources for employees in the computer field (MediaTec, 2002).

Many of the certifying organizations in the sample publish information regarding the dates they began offering the exams, but most do not. Nevertheless, through an examination of the organizations' Web sites (Table 3), I found that although some certifications were offered as early as 1930 (welding) and 1950 (finance), most were developed during the 1990s, and a significant number were developed between 2000 and 2003. The organizations indicated that they had experienced a rapid increase in the number of people certified per year during the 1990s.

***Implications for Practice.*** The increased use of certification has an impact on the human resource development field because it promotes the acceptance of nationally standardized bodies of knowledge. The result is that much of the training being offered in the United States is no longer customized to specific organizational needs. Employers are increasingly hiring employees who already have a great deal of knowledge in their fields. In-house training and development staff must therefore alter their curriculum away from offering organizational-specific training on an entire body of knowledge and instead offer training that focuses on how to transfer a generalized body of knowledge to an organization's needs. For example, rather than teaching a high school graduate all the knowledge needed to be a help desk employee at a particular bank, the trainer would teach a certified employee only the specific knowledge of an organization (for example, names of software and hardware used) that the certified employee would need to provide assistance to the bank's employees. In the long run, corporations may decrease their number of training and development staff, while certification organizations will increase their number of training and development staff.

**Summary of Findings.** Increased globalization, continued expansion of the service sector, and continued decline of the manufacturing sector during the 1990s led employers to demand a greater number of highly skilled employees. Employers became willing to accept new types of credentials (skill certification) in addition to their continued acceptance of college degrees. This increased demand for skilled employees induced several changes affecting the supply of skilled labor:

- There have been new government initiatives to increase the skill level of the U.S. labor force.
- There has been increased college attendance of young adults.
- There has been expanded development of skill certification exams by private organizations.
- There has been an increased number of employees obtaining skill certification.

**Limitations of the Study.** Despite the exponential growth in certifications, there has been little systematic tracking of the trend. The federal government data lack detail prior to the mid-1990s. It also would be helpful to know the Department of Labor and Department of Education policies and programs that were implemented and their impact on the certification arena. The sample relied on private, for-profit organizations that promote their certifications over the Internet, but it also would be worthwhile to determine the number of certifications offered by government programs, nonprofits, and colleges.

We do not know exactly how many certifications are available or how many people have been certified. Furthermore, we do not know the rigor of the certification exams or the accuracy of the certification exams for measuring skill sets. In short, although employees eagerly obtain certifications and employers willingly accept certifications as indicators of skill levels, we are left with the question: Is this an acceptable practice?

The following call for future research presents guidelines that can be used to answer this question.

## A Call for Future Research

Despite the exponential growth of the availability of certification during the 1990s, several key types of information are unknown:

The exact extent to which employees are obtaining certification is unknown. Although there has been an increase in demand for employees with high skills, it is unknown whether employees with certification receive more job offers or higher wages than those received by employees without certification (Herman, 1999; Silvestri, 1997; Braddock, 1999).

Whether employees with certification are indeed more highly skilled than are employees without certification is unknown.

This call for future research focuses on the last two areas.

***Effect of Certification on Labor Market Outcomes of Employees.*** If a particular certification is not legally required for entry into a field and the certification nevertheless improves labor market outcomes, then these improved labor market outcomes could be due to the knowledge, skills, and abilities attained while becoming certified or the prestige of being certified. That is, employers may simply believe certified employees are more highly skilled employees. A second issue to consider is the Pygmalion effect. That is, some trainees perform better before and after training than nontrainees perform because the trainees gain higher career expectations and self-efficacy by enrolling in training, regardless of the level of learning they achieve (Alampay & Morgan, 2000).

In order to determine whether certification improves labor market outcomes and whether the improvement is due to increased skills or increased prestige, researchers should compare employees who have been certified with employees who have not been certified on their educational and labor market characteristics. Such a study should survey employees regarding the extent of their education, training, and certification and regarding their employment and wages over time.

A time-series study should be conducted to determine the long-term effects of certification on labor market outcomes. This will enable researchers to determine whether certified employees are more successful than noncertified employees. It might be the case that certified employees are hired more readily, but that they do not advance in their careers faster than noncertified employees if their skills do not markedly differ from those of noncertified employees.

This study should measure employment variables that include industry occupation, wages, number of job offers, salaries offered, and job tenure for 1990–2004. The survey also should measure educational outcomes, including degrees earned and school name, certification earned and provider name, continuing education courses attended, on-the-job training, and self-study type and quantity. Demographic control variables should include, gender, age, ethnicity, geographical region, and national origin. The results of this study will indicate whether employees with certification are indeed more highly skilled than noncertified employees and the effects of certification on labor market outcomes.

*Reliability and Validity of Measurement of Skills.* The wide variety of sources of certifications makes it difficult for employers to gauge the merits of specific certifications, and some employers are wary of accepting certifications as meaningful credentials, while other employers accept all certifications at face value. In order for an organization to determine whether to use a certification test score as a selection device, it must know whether the knowledge, skills, and abilities purportedly measured through the certification are measured accurately (Pearlman, 1997; Schmitt, 1997; U.S. Department of Labor, 1978). Validity and reliability information would allow employers to choose among employees more accurately and would give employees clear explanations of what is required for success in the workplace, as well as the means to achieve a higher standard of living.

The mechanism to indicate the validity reliability of certifications can be provided through an examination of existing certifications according to guidelines developed by the Department of Labor (U.S. Department of Labor, 1978). This examination should consist of an analysis of the validity and reliability of the tests and the credential-granting processes.

*Reliability.* Researchers should first determine whether the certification exams measure consistently. Researchers should examine the test-retest reliability to determine whether the exams produce similar results over repeated testings. If there is more than one version of a specific test (as there are for many), researchers should conduct parallel forms study to determine whether different versions of the same test produce similar results. For tests that require subjective grading (such as interviews or essays), researchers should examine the interrater reliability to determine whether the exams produce similar results across raters (Carmines & Zeller, 1979; Cohen, 1987).

*Validity.* Following the reliability studies, researchers should determine whether the inferences drawn from the exams are accurate. For example, they should examine the content validity of exams to determine whether the importance of subtopics on exams accurately reflects the importance of these subtopics to job content. They also should examine the internal consistency of exams to determine whether the exams measure what they purport to measure. For example, does the Certified Payroll Professional exam measure only knowledge of payroll functions, or does it also measure other types of human resource knowledge? Finally, researchers should examine the criterion-related validity of the instruments to determine whether test scores accurately predict job performance.

*Difficulties Developing Advanced Skills Standards and Certification Exams.* It is important to examine the validity and reliability of certification exams because these standards are difficult and expensive to develop. The difficulty and expense stem from the fact that certification standards measure skills (that is, the ability to perform a task), not knowledge needed to perform a task (Gerber, 1995). That is, although it is difficult to measure a body of knowledge with a written test, it is far more difficult to measure a set of skills with a written test (Nunnally, 1978). Many skills are best measured through measuring the performance of tasks rather than through measuring the knowledge used in performing those tasks (Carter, 2001; Osburn, 1987).

In addition, it is difficult to determine which set of skills should be combined into standards for a given occupation (Milkovich & Newman, 1999). Several organizations have experienced difficulty developing job and skill standards. For example, after receiving a grant from the NSSB, the National Retail Federation worked for nearly two years to develop standards for the position of sales associate (Gerber, 1995). A second example can be drawn from the United Kingdom, which found the development of skills standards to be prohibitively expensive (Gerber, 1995). A third example can be drawn from the American Electronics Association, which represents three thousand U.S.-based technology companies and which took nearly six years to develop standards. The association received a $279,000 NSSB grant in 1996 to develop a set of standards to help employers and community colleges design training and curriculum. By 1998, it had developed guidelines that could be used to create skills standards yet had not implemented the guidelines and subsequently reported to Congress regarding a continued shortage of skilled electrical and computer employees (Hughlett, 1999). Subsequently, five organizations developed electronics skills standards and certifications under the auspices of the NSSB (NSSB, 2002b). In sum, given the difficulty and expense of creating standards, it is important to know whether these standards are reliable and valid. More important, it is crucial to determine whether certifications improve labor market outcomes for employees.

## Conclusions

The United States experienced striking changes in its industrial mix, technology, and educational legislation during the 1990s. These changes combined to pressure the U.S. educational system to adopt new models of delivering skills and credentials. One major change in the U.S. educational system was the increased reliance on, and prestige of, certification. Employers have been increasingly seeking employees with a skill level between a high school diploma and a bachelor's degree and have been filling this need by hiring employees with certifications as opposed to training all employees in-house. The occupations for which these skill levels are relevant are projected to continue to grow rapidly during the next decade, making it more important than ever before for researchers to determine the validity of certifications and the full effects of certification on labor market outcomes.

## References

Adelman, C. (2000). *A parallel postsecondary universe: The certification system in informational technology.* Washington, DC: U.S. Department of Education, Office of Educational Research and Improvement.

Alampay, R. H., & Morgan, F. T. (2000). Evaluating external executive education at Dow Chemical: Its impact and the Pygmalion effect. *Human Resource Development International, 3,* 489–498.

Bellinger, R. (1996, July 15). Seeks to create performance measurements for manufacturing, support personnel—AEA receives workplace skills grant. *Electronic Engineering Times,* 76.

Bishop, J. H. (1993). Underinvestment in employer training: A mandate to spend? *Human Resource Development Quarterly, 4,* 223–241.

Bishop, J. H. (1996). Is the market for college graduates headed for a bust? Demand and supply responses to rising college wage premiums. *New England Economic Review, 21,* 115–136.

Bishop, J. H., & Carter, S. D. (1991). The worsening shortage of college graduate employees. *Education Evaluation and Policy Analysis, 13,* 221–246.

Braddock, D. (1999). Occupational employment projections to 2008. *Monthly Labor Review, 120* (11), 51–77.

Carmines, E. G., & Zeller, R. A. (1979). *Reliability and validity assessment.* Thousand Oaks, CA: Sage.

Carter, S. D. (2001). Assessment. In J. Michie (Ed.), *Reader's guide to the social sciences.* London: Fitzroy Dearborn.

Charters, M. (1999, March 1). Hitting the books. *Publishers Weekly,* 37.

Cohen, J. (1987). *Statistical power analysis for the behavioral sciences* (rev. ed.). Mahwah, NJ: Erlbaum.

Cook, T. D., & Campbell, D. T. (1979). *Quasi-experimentation: Design and analysis issues for field settings.* Boston: Houghton Mifflin.

Dilworth, R. L. (2001). Shaping HRD for the new millennium. *Human Resource Development Quarterly, 12,* 103–104.

Eck, A. (1993). Job-related education and training: Their impact on earnings. *Monthly Labor Review, 116* (10), 21–40.

Ehrenberg, R. G., & Smith, R. S. (2000). *Modern labor economics: Theory and public policy.* Reading, MA: Addison-Wesley.

Fellerton, H. N. (1989). New labor force projections spanning 1988 to 2000. *Monthly Labor Review, 112* (11), 3–12.

Garavaglia, P. L. (1993). How to ensure transfer of training. *Training and Development, 47* (10), 63–68.

Gerber, B. (1995). The plan to certify America (standard setting and certification of occupations). *Training, 32* (2), 39–45.

Hecker, D. E. (2001). Occupational employment projections to 2010. *Monthly Labor Review, 124* (11), 57–84.

Herman, A. M. (1999). *Report on the American workforce.* Washington, DC: U.S. Department of Labor.

Hight, J. E. (1998). Young worker participation in post-school education and training. *Monthly Labor Review, 121* (6), 14–23.

Hughlett, R. (1999, October 29). Worker shortage takes toll on high-tech firms. *Baltimore Business Journal,* 22.

Katz, S., Hwang, J., & Resnick, L. B. (1997). *Creating skill standards for the high performance workplace.* Washington, DC: National Skill Standards Board.

Kaufman, P., Kwon, J. Y., Klein, S., & Chapman, C. D. (1999). *Dropout rates in the United States: 1998.* Washington, DC: U.S. Department of Education, Office of Educational Research and Improvement.

Kirkpatrick, D. L. (1998). *Evaluating training programs: The four levels* (2nd ed.). San Francisco: Berrett-Koehler.

Krenek, D. (2000, March 11). Trade up to vocational ed. *New York Daily News,* 16.

Lauer, C. (2002). Enrolments in higher education: Do economic incentives matter? *Education and Training, 44,* 179–185.

MediaTec. (2002). *About MediaTec Publishing, Inc.* San Francisco: MediaTec Publishing. [http://www.certmag.com/common/whoismt.cfm].

Milkovich, G. T., & Newman, J. M. (1999). *Compensation* (6th ed.). New York: McGraw-Hill.

National Skills Standards Board. (2002a). *The NSSB: A brief description.* Washington, DC: Author. [http://www.nssb.org/].

National Skills Standards Board. (2002b). *Industry coalitions.* Washington, DC: Author. [http://www.nssb.org/].

National Skills Standards Board. (2003). *Certifications and apprenticeships.* Washington, DC: Author. [http://www.nssb.org/].

Nunnally, J. C. (1978). *Psychometric theory.* New York: McGraw-Hill.

Osburn, H. G. (1987). Personnel selection. In G. Salvendy (Ed.), *Handbook of human factors.* New York: Wiley.

Pearlman, K. (1997). *Standards for standards: Recommended National Skill Standards Board Criteria for Describing Work, Performance, and Standards.* Washington, DC: National Skill Standards Board.

Pierce, D. R. (2000, March 6). College alternative. *USA Today,* 14A.

Schmitt, N. (1997). *Standards for assessing competence.* Washington, DC: National Skill Standards Board.

Silverberg, M., Warner, E., Goodwin, D., & Fong, M. (2002). *National assessment of vocational education: Interim report to congress.* Washington, DC: U.S. Department of Education, Office of the Under Secretary.

Silvestri, G. T. (1993). Occupational employment: Wide variations in growth. *Monthly Labor Review, 116* (11), 58–86.

Silvestri, G. T. (1995). Occupational employment to 2005. *Monthly Labor Review, 118* (11), 60–87.

Silvestri, G. T. (1997). Occupational employment projections to 2006. *Monthly Labor Review, 120* (11), 58–83.

Silvestri, G. T., & Lukasiewicz, J. (1991). Occupation employment projections. *Monthly Labor Review, 114* (11), 64–94.

Snyder, T. D., & Hoffman, C. M. (2003). *Digest of education statistics, 2002.* Washington, DC: U.S. Department of Education, National Center for Educational Statistics.

Thurow, L. C. (1997). The rise and fall of brain power. *Industry Week, 246* (11), 114–118.

U.S. Congress. (1991, April 18). President Bush's new education strategy. *Congressional Record,* p. S4724. [http://thomas.loc.gov/cgi-bin/query/D?r102:1:./temp/~r102l9m1nq::].

U.S. Congress. (1992, July 22). The Bush education record. *Congressional Record,* p. S10148. [http://thomas.loc.gov/cgi-bin/query/D?r102:1:./temp/~r10225Dl4c::].

U.S. Congress. (1994a, February 8). Goals 2000: Educate America Act. *Congressional Record,* p. S1146. [http://thomas.loc.gov/cgi-bin/query/D?r103:7:./temp/~r103Df636H::].

U.S. Congress. (1994b, March 23). Conference report on H.R. 1804, Goals 2000: Educate America Act. *Congressional Record,* p. H1921. [http://thomas.loc.gov/cgi-bin/query/D?r103:3:./temp/ ~r103EODW9N::].

U.S. Congress. (1994c, April 12). Bills and a joint resolution presented to the president. *Congressional Record,* p. H2215. [http://thomas.loc.gov/cgi-bin/query/D?r103:4:./temp/ ~r103nFQmbD::].

U.S. Department of Commerce. (2000). *Years of school completed by people 25 years old and over, by age and sex: Selected years 1940 to 1999.* [http://www.census.gov/population/socdemo/ education/tableA-1.txt].

U.S. Department of Labor. (1978). *Code of federal regulations: 41 CFR chapter 60, part 60–3—uniform guidelines on employee selection procedures.* Washington, DC: U.S. Government Printing Office.

U.S. Department of Labor. (1998). *Occupational outlook handbook.* Washington, DC: U.S. Government Printing Office.

U.S. Department of Labor. (2002, August 2). *The employment situation: July 2002.* Washington, DC: U.S. Department of Labor. [ftp://ftp.bls.gov/pub/news.release/History/empsit.08022002.news].

U.S. Department of Labor and U.S. Department of Commerce. (1996). *Annual demographic survey (March CPS supplement): Methodology and documentation.* Washington, DC: U.S. Department of Labor and U.S. Department of Commerce. [http://www.bls.census.gov/cps/ads/1996/sglosary.htm].

Veum, J. R. (1993). Training among young adults: Who, what kind, and for how long? *Monthly Labor Review, 116* (8), 27–34.

Wash, D. P. (1995–1996). A new way to classify occupations by education and training. *Occupational Outlook Quarterly, 39* (4), 28–40.

Young, M. W. (1993). National priorities for education: A conversation with U.S. Secretary of Education Richard W. Riley. *National Forum, 73* (4), 5–7.

*Shani D. Carter is assistant professor in the Department of Management, School of Management and Technology, at Rhode Island College in Providence.*

For bulk reprints of this article, please call (201) 748-8789.

# Development and Validation of the Learning Transfer System Inventory in Taiwan

*Hsin-Chih Chen, E. F. Holton III, Reid Bates*

*Due to globalization in recent years, organizations and the government in Taiwan take developing human expertise more seriously than ever before. However, human resource development evaluation practices in Taiwan have somewhat overlooked connecting training to transfer and organizational results. To help close the gap, organizations in Taiwan need a valid and reliable instrument to assess transfer issues. This study validated a research-based instrument in the United States, the Learning Transfer System Inventory (LTSI), for use in Taiwan. A heterogeneous sample containing 583 responses from twenty organizations was collected. Through a rigorous translation process with qualitatively subjective, quantitatively objective, and pilot evaluations of the translation as well as common factor analyses, a Taiwan version of the LTSI (TLTSI), which contained fifteen statistically reliable factors, was validated. This study also extended the LTSI's generalizability and provided comparable measures of transfer systems between Taiwan and the United States. Translation issues, suggestions for improving the LTSI, implications for HRD, and future research directions are discussed.*

Human resource development (HRD) is a relatively new profession but not a new concept in Taiwan. A review of the history of HRD in Taiwan vividly illustrates that it has been embedded in the government's human resource policy and linked to economic growth since 1953. The Taiwanese government has long perceived that developing highly competent human resources will lead to economic growth (Kuo & McLean, 1999).

HRD has been instrumental in Taiwan's economic miracle in Asia since the 1960s. According to the global competitiveness report of the World Economic Forum, published by the Center for International Development at Harvard University, Taiwan, among over one hundred economies, was ranked third in economic growth in 2002 (Cornelius, 2003) and fifth in 2003 (Schwab, 2004).

HUMAN RESOURCE DEVELOPMENT QUARTERLY, vol. 16, no. 1, Spring 2005
Copyright © 2005 Wiley Periodicals, Inc.

Taiwan was also top-ranked in the Asian region for both years. Yuen (1994) asserted that Taiwan's government has created technical training and vocational schools that have dramatically enhanced workers' skills, knowledge, and abilities. The government's emphasis on developing human resources has led Taiwan to become one of the most powerful economies in the world. Although other factors, such as government financial policies and market forces, have influenced Taiwan's economic growth, the government policies that highly value human capital point to the contribution of HRD to this growth. Indeed, in a country such as Taiwan with limited natural resources, human capital is a more vital concept than in countries with abundant natural resources, such as the United States and China.

Due to the new era of globalization, organizations in Taiwan have been facing more rigorous competition than ever before. As a result, HRD has received additional attention in both the public and private sectors. In the public sector, Taiwan's government has embedded the concept of HRD in the government transformation process. One of the most dramatic government policies putting the HRD concept into action has been the legislation referred to as the Civil Servant Life-Long Learning Act (LY 01765)(2002). The vision of this legislation is to build an integrated human resource system by promoting innovation, continual learning, and self-management learning to improve the quality of civil services to citizens in a more effective and efficient fashion, with an ultimate goal of building a learning government.

In the private sector, training has been a prevalent concern for organization decision makers. A major industrial and business magazine, *Common Wealth*, conducted a nationwide study ranking the top one thousand companies in Taiwan and surveyed their business priorities (Chuang, 1998). The top two priorities of those companies were training and development and research and development; indeed, 47.8 percent of these top organizations perceived that training and development was the highest priority they needed to address.

## Research Problem

Despite the fact that organizations in Taiwan highly value HRD, training evaluation practices there still fall short in measuring transfer and organizational results (Lin & Chiu, 1997). Because training is one way to develop human resources and facilitating transfer of learning is an approach to help unleash human expertise, it seems clear that both should be equally important to HRD in Taiwan. In order to demonstrate HRD's effectiveness, organizations in Taiwan need valid tools to assess transfer interventions and performance results. However, assessing the effectiveness of coherent transfer interventions requires a valid instrument. Unfortunately, although some research has been done on assessing transfer issues in Taiwan (Chuo, 1997; Chen, 1997), none of it has focused on developing a generalizable instrument to assess factors affecting transfer of training. In addition, these studies have been limited because only a few factors were investigated and the generalizability of these studies is weak because of the small sample sizes. Therefore, developing a comprehensive, generalizable, valid instrument of learning transfer will help organizations in Taiwan effectively and efficiently manage transfer interventions by diagnosing the strengths and weaknesses of their learning transfer systems.

Models or reviews identifying factors affecting transfer of training or training effectiveness have been abundant (Baldwin & Ford, 1988; Ford & Weissbein, 1997; Kabanoff & Bottger, 1991; Kraiger, Ford, & Salas, 1993; Holton, 1996; Noe, 1986; Noe & Schmitt, 1986; Steiner, Dobbins, & Trahan, 1991). However, most of the models do not provide psychometrically sound measurement scales. A search of the literature related to transfer of training turned up the Learning Transfer System Inventory (LTSI) as the only research-based instrument for assessing factors affecting transfer of learning (Holton, Bates, & Ruona, 2000). The LTSI appears to be comprehensive because it covers sixteen factors related to transfer of training. It has also exhibited evidence of generalizability due to heterogeneous sample that was used. Holton et al. (2000) collected data from 1,616 subjects who attended nine different training programs from government, public for-profit, private, and nonprofit organizations. The training programs included in the study were either knowledge based (for example, customer service and professional training) or skill based (for example, clerical and technical skills). However, none of the subjects was collected from affective-related training.

Cross-cultural research to compare similarities and differences across cultures or nations has been abundant in some areas (Hendriks et al., 2003; Hofstede, 2001; Jackson, 2001). However, research in comparing transfer of learning across cultures or nations is still in its infancy. Because cross-cultural studies have found that some psychological constructs vary across different cultures (Hofstede, 2001), there is a need to validate the LTSI through translation, so practitioners and researchers will have access to sound psychometric quality scales to compare transfer of learning factors and their relationship to performance-related measures across cultures.

Thus, the purpose of this study was to conduct a rigorous translation of the LTSI, validate the LTSI in Taiwan's organizations, and develop an instrument of transfer of learning that is statistically reliable and valid for use in Taiwan in order to address the research problems just described. The research questions were as follows:

1. Through a series of translation, evaluation processes, and factor analysis, how many factors from the original LTSI are valid for use in Taiwan's organizations?
2. Twenty-one new items, designed by the original LTSI authors were added to current LTSI for the purpose of improving the reliabilities of the five problematic factors. When including these items in another factor analysis with the data, will more valid factors be found and the reliabilities of these factors be improved?

3. If affective-related data are collected, will the data suggest that the LTSI can be used to measure transfer issues for affective-related training?
4. Will this study be able to provide comparable transfer factors for a cross-culture study between Taiwan and the United States?

## Review of Literature

This section introduces the LTSI theoretical framework, reviews studies related to previous LTSI development and validity, and reviews approaches for cross-cultural instrument translation.

*Theoretical Framework of the LTSI.* The LTSI has four sets of factors: motivation, work environment, ability, and secondary influences (also known as trainee characteristics). The motivation, work environment, and ability factors directly influence individual performance, whereas the secondary influences are perceived to affect motivation and then further to affect individual performance. The conceptual framework is shown in Figure 1. The definitions, reliabilities of the factors, and sample items for the LTSI are provided in Table 1.

**Figure 1. Learning Transfer System Inventory: Conceptual Model of Instrument Constructs**

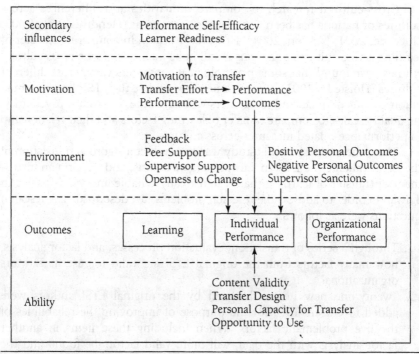

*Source:* Holton, Bates, & Ruona (2000, p. 239).

**Table 1. English LTSI Scale Definitions and Sample Items**

| Factor | Definition | Sample Item | Number of Items | α |
|---|---|---|---|---|
| **TRAINING SPECIFIC SCALES** | | | | |
| Learner Readiness | The extent to which individuals are prepared to enter and participate in training. | Before the training I had a good understanding of how it would fit my job-related development. | 4 | .73 |
| Motivation to Transfer | The direction, intensity, and persistence of effort toward utilizing in a work setting skills and knowledge learned. | I get excited when I think about trying to use my new learning on my job. | 4 | .83 |
| Positive Personal Outcomes | The degree to which applying training on the job leads to outcomes that are positive for the individual. | Employees in this organization receive various "perks" when they utilize newly learned skills on the job. | 3 | .69 |
| Negative Personal Outcomes | The extent to which individuals believe that not applying skills and knowledge learned in training will lead to outcomes that are negative. | If I do not utilize my training I will be cautioned about it. | 4 | .76 |
| Personal Capacity for Transfer | The extent to which individuals have the time, energy and mental space in their work lives to make changes required to transfer learning to the job. | My workload allows me time to try the new things I have learned. | 4 | .68 |
| Peer Support | The extent to which peers reinforce and support use of learning on the job. | My colleagues encourage me to use the skills I have learned in training. | 4 | .83 |
| Supervisor Support | The extent to which supervisors-managers support and reinforce use of training on the job. | My supervisor sets goals for me, which encourage me to apply my training on the job. | 6 | .91 |
| Supervisor Sanctions | The extent to which individuals perceive negative responses from supervisors-managers when applying skills learned in training. | My supervisor opposes the use of the techniques I learned in training. | 3 | .63 |
| Perceived Content Validity | The extent to which trainees judge training content to accurately reflect job requirements. | What is taught in training closely matches my job requirements. | 5 | .84 |

*(Continued)*

**Table 1. English LTSI Scale Definitions and Sample Items (Continued)**

| Factor | Definition | Sample Item | Number of Items | α |
|---|---|---|---|---|
| Transfer Design | Degree to which (1) training has been designed and delivered to give trainees the ability to transfer learning to the job, and (2) training instructions match job requirements. | The activities and exercises the trainers used helped me know how to apply my learning on the job. | 4 | .85 |
| Opportunity to Use | The extent to which trainees are provided with or obtain resources and tasks on the job enabling them to use training on the job. | The resources I need to use what I learned will be available to me after training. | 4 | .70 |
| GENERAL SCALES | | | | |
| Transfer Effort– Performance Expectations | The expectation that effort devoted to transferring learning will lead to changes in job performance. | My job performance improves when I use new things that I have learned. | 4 | .81 |
| Performance- Outcomes Expectations | The expectation that changes in job performance will lead to valued outcomes. | When I do things to improve my performance, good things happen to me. | 5 | .83 |
| Resistance/ Openness to Change | The extent to which prevailing group norms are perceived by individuals to resist or discourage the use of skills and knowledge acquired in training. | People in my group are open to changing the way they do things. | 6 | .85 |
| Performance Self-Efficacy | An individual's general belief that they are able to change their performance when they want to. | I am confident in my ability to use newly learned skills on the job. | 4 | .76 |
| Performance Coaching | Formal and informal indicators from an organization about an individual's job performance. | After training, I get feedback from people about how well I am applying what I learned. | 4 | .70 |

*Source:* Holton, Bates, & Ruona (2000, pp. 344–346).

Sixty-eight items measuring sixteen factors represent two construct domains: Training in Specific and Training in General in the LTSI. The Training in Specific domain contains forty-five items measuring eleven constructs. The Training in General domain consists of twenty-three items measuring five constructs.

*Development and Validity of the LTSI.* A number of studies (Holton, Chen, & Naquin, 2003; Bates & Holton, 2004) have used the LTSI in different settings. This section does not look at all of the studies using LTSI as the instrument. Rather, the focus is on studies that demonstrate the psychometric qualities of the LTSI.

In early development of the LTSI, Holton, Bates, Seyler, and Carvalho (1997) factor-analyzed nine constructs for transfer climate. The factors assessed in the study were essentially related to environmental factors. Holton et al. (2000) expanded the instrument by fitting the factors to an evaluation model (Holton, 1996) and included motivational-related (for example, expectancy and motivation to transfer), ability-related (for example, personal capacity for transfer), and trainee-characteristics-related factors (for example, learner readiness and performance self-efficacy) to the previous version of the instrument. With a heterogeneous sample, the results suggested that sixteen LTSI factors were validated. Yamnill (2001) conducted a construct validation study of the LTSI in Thailand and found that it was valid for use there. Bookter (1999) conducted a divergent and convergent validity of the LTSI, suggesting that it contains unique constructs and concluded that it is divergent to other known constructs relating to transfer of learning.

In addition, three studies that focused on criterion validity of the LTSI suggested that environmental factors, especially for interpersonal supports, are the most powerful predictors of individual performance (Bates, Holton, & Seyler, 1997; Bates, Holton, Seyler, & Carvalho, 2000) and motivation to transfer (Seyler, Holton, Bates, Burnett, & Carvalho, 1998). Another criterion validity study of the LTSI (Ruona, Leimbach, Holton, & Bates, 2002) suggested that reaction utility might be indirectly related to performance but directly related to motivation to transfer.

*Translation Approaches for Cross-Cultural Studies.* There are three types of development strategies for cross-cultural instruments: one-shot translation, forward-back translation, and simultaneous instrument development (Bullinger, Anderson, Cella, & Aronson, 1993; Brislin, 1970; Hui & Triandis, 1985). The one-shot translation, also known as forward-only translation, is the least rigorous and least valid approach. It refers to direct literal translation from an original language to a target language without any evaluation of the translation.

The forward-back translation approaches start with the forward translation, and the instrument is then back-translated to the original language for an evaluation of the translation in the native language. The forward-back-translation approaches have two subtypes: sequential and parallel. Direct translation and evaluation process are involved, and no change is made to the original instrument in the sequential forward-back translation. For the parallel forward-back approach, the original instrument can be adjusted in order to reduce language limitations as well as to make the original and the translated instrument as comparable as possible. Finally, the simultaneous approach generally does not involve questionnaire translation but identification of appropriate factors that are perceived to be cross-culturally valid. Based on the predetermined factors, the instruments are then developed separately in local languages.

## Method

This section describes the version of the LTSI used in this study and the translation process conducted in this study. It then addresses research design, population, sample, and implementation.

*Instrumentation.* The version of the LTSI used in this study contained sixty-eight validated items plus twenty-one research items that the authors tested to improve lower reliabilities of five constructs: Positive Personal Outcomes, alpha = .69; Personal Capacity for Transfer, alpha = .68; Supervisor Sanction, alpha = .63; Opportunity to Use Learning, alpha = .70; and Performance Coaching, alpha = .70). All of the items used a Likert-type scale ranging from 1 (Strongly Disagree) to 5 (Strongly Agree). Because the quality of translation is the key to ensuring the functional equivalence between the two versions of the LTSI, a forward-back translation with subjective, objective, and pilot evaluations was used to create the Taiwan version of the LTSI.

Chen (2003) distinguished two concepts in the translation process: identical translation and functional equivalence translation. Identical translation refers to translation that produces an instrument as close to the original as possible. It focuses on identical word-by-word translation and maintains the original sentence structure (such as subject-verb structure), so it has a potential threat to validity in that the meaning may be distorted in the translation process. The functional equivalence translation focuses on two criteria: equivalence of meaning and use of commonly used words in the target language. The equivalence of meaning will ensure that sentences are not misinterpreted, and the commonly used words in the target language assist in readability and functionality of the translated instrument in the target language.

*Sequential Forward-Back Translation.* Because the English version of the LTSI had been previously validated, any changes to the original may alter the factor structure. Therefore, sequential forward-back translation strategy was appropriate and adopted in this study. Two bilingual translators (one was the first author of this article) separately translated the English version of the LTSI to Mandarin Chinese. (Both translators had received graduate HRD degrees in the United States.) They attempted to retain the form and the meaning of the items as close to the original as possible, and they agreed to use common language in the translation. When they completed the translation, they compared their translated instruments item by item to assess the consistency of the translation. Items with disagreement or errors were further discussed and revised until both translators reached a consensus.

A first draft version of Taiwan's LTSI (TLTSI) was then finalized and labeled the TLTSI draft. A bilingual translator, who had never seen the LTSI before and had strong language skills in both English and Mandarin Chinese, then translated the TLTSI draft back to English. (The back translator is a faculty member in a social science–related field in a major university in the United States.)

*Subjective Evaluation.* The back translation was then reviewed by one of the original LTSI authors to evaluate the English LTSI to the English back-translated version of the TLTSI draft. The primary focus in this step was to make sure that the meanings of the LTSI items were equivalent in both English versions. Problematic items were sent back through entire process; they were retranslated, back-translated, and reviewed by the LTSI author again. This process continued until no items exhibited substantial differences that could be found by the LTSI author. This version was then labeled the *TLTSI back.*

*Objective Evaluation.* According to Sperber, Devellis, and Boehlecke (1994), the success of translation in most cross-cultural studies is based on the translator's satisfaction; relatively few have been done through an objective evaluation. As a check on the possible individual bias of the LTSI author, a quantitative approach of evaluation through an objective lens was also conducted in this study. The purpose of this evaluation was to test the quality of the transition by again evaluating the two English versions: the original LTSI and the TLTSI back.

Two measures, comparability of language and similarity of interpretability, were assessed. The former assesses the similarity of words, phrases, and sentences, while the latter assesses the similarity of an item's meaning. An instrument using a Likert-type scale ranging from 1 (Extremely Comparable/Similar) to 7 (Not at All Comparable/Similar) was developed for this step. A survey instrument was developed that contained the two English versions of the items (original wording and TLTSI back wording) along with the rating scales. This survey was distributed to a group of HRD graduate students and experienced trainers. All of them were English monolingual raters. Eighteen individuals received the instrument, and fifteen of the responses were returned; thirteen were useable. A 3.0 criterion was set to determine the effect of the two measures. Scores above 3.0 indicated potential problematic items.

In terms of the comparability of language measure, the results showed that fifteen items had mean values greater than 3.0, indicating that the wordings of these items were not comparable. However, on the similarity of interpretability measure, the results showed that only eight items had mean values greater than 3.0. The similarity of interpretability measure became the primary focus of the translation because it assesses equivalence of meaning and the Mandarin language forces some sentence forms that appear awkward to English readers when back-translated. The eight items with mean values of similarity of interpretability measure greater than 3.0 were examined further. None of them had a mean value greater than 4.0. A closer examination of these items suggested that problems with these items were due to differences between the two different languages, so no further revision was possible.

*Pilot Test.* The TLTSI was sent to nine HRD practitioners in Taiwan to collect feedback on whether the instrument and its instructions were understandable and the technical terms in the instrument were interpretable in Taiwan. All of the selected practitioners had HRD work experience of more than five years and were trainers, human resource consultants, or HR managers. The pilot test was a checkpoint for the readability and functionality of the translated instrument. The comments provided by these HRD practitioners indicated that the instrument seemed appropriate for use in Taiwan except for some concerns about the length and similar items in the instrument. However, the similar items were the research items intended to improve the reliability of the lower reliability scales. The length of the instrument was not changed due to multiple purposes of this study. Therefore, all eighty-nine items were retained and distributed.

*Research Design, Population, Sample, and Implementation.* This study was a nonexperimental survey design. The target population was employees who attended training programs within or outside their organization and provided by trainers in Taiwan. In terms of sampling techniques, probability sampling would exhibit stronger validity than nonprobability sampling (Ary, Jacobs, & Razavieh, 1996). Probability included four types—simple random, stratified, cluster, and systematic sampling—while the nonprobability sampling contains accidental, purposive, and quota samplings. These sampling techniques were deliberately considered. However, because a roster of all trainees in Taiwan does not exist, the simple random and systematic sampling techniques could not be done. Although stratified or cluster samplings could be done by selecting a sample from a list of organizations in Taiwan, these approaches did not fit the purposes of this study. This is because there would be no control on availability of training and types of training provided by the selected organizations. Therefore, nonprobability sampling was used, and a combination of purposive and accidental samplings was appropriate because the quota sampling also did not fit the research purposes.

The first author attended two international HRD-related conferences in 2002 to solicit Taiwan's HRD practitioners to participate in this study. More than sixty practitioners from Taiwan attended the conferences in 2002. In addition, the researcher visited Taiwan to obtain additional participants. The sampling frame included employees who received training from these HRD practitioners' affiliated organizations. Predetermined criteria for subject selection were to collect data in the sampling frame that would represent different organizations, organizational types, and training types as possible.

Thirteen HRD practitioners agreed to serve as instrument administrators and helped distribute the instrument in their organizations. Each practitioner received an administration guide and thirty to one hundred instruments. The guide contained information about the research purpose, contents of the instrument, target respondents, distribution timing, and issues about confidentiality. The number of instruments disseminated in an organization depended on its size, trainee accessibility, variety of training programs conducted, and organizational type. The first author also scheduled a one-month trip in Taiwan to deal with administration issues. Participation was on a voluntary and anonymous basis.

Some instrument administrators who served in public training institutes were able to distribute instruments to participants from more than one organization. The data were collected from trainees either immediately after the training or no later than two weeks after training. Due to anonymous participation, no follow-up was conducted with trainees.

There were 712 instruments distributed and 583 responses collected from twenty organizations, for an 82 percent response rate. These organizations represented public sector ($N = 77$, 13.3 percent), private sector ($N = 267$, 46.3 percent), educational institutes ($N = 59$, 10.2 percent), public for-profit ($N = 63$, 0.9 percent), and nonprofit ($N = 100$, 17.3 percent) organizations. There were 577 usable responses. A sample description can be found in Table 2.

*Analysis.* Two major factor analysis techniques were considered: exploratory factor analysis (EFA) and confirmatory factor analysis (CFA). The CFA is more appropriate when a study is supported by strong theory. CFA would have been an adequate technique to use if it was known that there were no variations among psychological constructs across countries, but that would be a weak assumption in this study. Because the theoretical framework of the LTSI had not been tested in Taiwan, EFA seemed more appropriate than CFA. Therefore, the exploratory common factor analysis with oblique rotation was used in this study. Oblique rotation was appropriate because interfactor relationship is assumed (Tabachnick & Fidell, 1996).

Before the EFA was conducted, visual normality and suitability for factor analysis were examined using procedures from Hair, Anderson, Tatham, and Black (1998). Following the English-language validation procedure, two separate exploratory factor analyses were run for the Training in Specific and Training in General domains (Holton et al., 2000). The number of factors to extract was based on a combination of an eigenvalue greater than one criterion and examination of scree plot. A .40 cutoff was the criterion to determine the number of items to retain in a factor for each of the EFA analyses.

## Results

No serious violation was found in the visual normality examination. The overall Kaiser's measure of sampling adequacy was .932, which means the data were appropriate for an exploratory common factor analysis. Responses to item ratios for all of the EFAs described in later in this section ranged from 7.9 to 1 to 22.1 to 1.

## Table 2. Sample Information by Organization and by Training by Organization

| | Frequency | Percentage | Cumulative Percentage |
|---|---|---|---|
| By organization | | | |
| Organization not identified | 22 | 3.8 | 3.8 |
| Civil service[a] | 57 | 9.9 | 13.7 |
| Education[b] | 58 | 10.1 | 23.8 |
| Electronic | 63 | 10.9 | 34.7 |
| Insurance[c] | 76 | 13.2 | 47.9 |
| Petroleum | 62 | 10.7 | 58.6 |
| Retail | 48 | 8.3 | 66.9 |
| Social work | 100 | 17.3 | 84.2 |
| Telecommunication | 60 | 10.4 | 94.6 |
| Transportation | 16 | 2.8 | 97.4 |
| Others[d] | 14 | 2.4 | 99.8 |
| Total | 577 | 99.8 | |
| By training | | | |
| Training type not identified | 98 | 17.0 | 17.0 |
| Computer skill training | 19 | 3.3 | 20.3 |
| Curriculum development | 30 | 5.2 | 25.5 |
| Customer service | 17 | 2.9 | 28.4 |
| Middle-level managerial training | 12 | 2.1 | 30.5 |
| New employee training | 52 | 9.0 | 39.5 |
| Machine maintenance, merchandise introduction, and customer satisfaction | 48 | 8.3 | 47.8 |
| Quality management | 12 | 2.1 | 49.9 |
| Safety training | 38 | 6.6 | 56.5 |
| Spiritual inspiration | 99 | 17.2 | 73.7 |
| System operation and accounting management | 27 | 4.7 | 78.4 |
| Train the trainer | 10 | 1.7 | 80.1 |
| Others[e] | 115 | 19.9 | 100.0 |
| Total | 577 | 100.0 | |

[a]Data collected from three civil service agencies.
[b]Data collected from three educational institutes.
[c]Data collected from two insurance companies.
[d]Six organizations with fewer than ten respondents are classified as "others."
[e]A variety of training programs with fewer than ten respondents classified as "others."

**Research Question 1.** Initial analyses were conducted using only the sixty-eight previously validated items. The results of the EFA showed that eleven of the sixteen LTSI factors were validated, and six were in need of further investigation (five for Training in Specific and one for Training in General domains). The six factors included two that did not emerge at all (Personal Capacity for Transfer and Performance Coaching), two that merged to a new factor

(Perceived Content Validity and Transfer Design), one that contained only two items (Supervisor Sanction; alpha = .66), and one with only one item (Opportunity to Use Learning). Due to space limitation, the result of this analysis was incorporated with other research questions (see Table 6).

*Research Question 2.* Cross-cultural instrument validation such as was done in this study is involved not only in cultural issues, but also in translation, implementation, and reliability issues. Each issue should be carefully examined before decisions are made about construct validity. Before concluding that the six factors were not valid in Taiwan, we decided to conduct additional analyses, including the twenty-one research items (eight-nine items in total) even though they had not been validated in the United States. We developed the following reasons for this addition.

First, as the analysis of research question 1 indicated, four of the six factors (Personal Capacity for Transfer, Supervisor Sanction, Opportunity to Use Learning, and Performance Coaching) that did not show initial construct validity in Taiwan matched the low reliability factors in the original LTSI. This raised our suspicion that items in the previously problematic factors might have affected the results. It would be premature to conclude that factors such as Personal Capacity for Transfer and Performance Coaching did not exist without careful further examination, especially since the weaknesses in these scales might have been magnified by the translation process. In addition, one of the purposes of this study was to develop an instrument of transfer of learning that is statistically reliable and valid for use in Taiwan. Thus, it made more sense to develop the best possible instrument for use in Taiwan, which meant examining the research items to see if the troublesome factors could be strengthened. If the troublesome factors remained problematic, then the conclusion that certain constructs do not exist in Taiwan can be made more confidently. But if problem factors were strengthened or reemerged when the research items were included, then it seems likely that the problems may have occurred due to translation or other artifacts but not true cultural differences. This is especially true when one considers that four of the six problem factors had been identified as having some weakness in the English language version also.

The procedures and criteria for the extended analysis were the same as those conducted in research question 1 except for having the research items included. In the Training in Specific domain, sixty-three items were used. These items included forty-five validated items and eighteen research items. Although the ratio of respondents to items in this analysis dropped to 9.2 to 1, it was still an acceptable ratio for factor analysis (Hair et al., 1998). Kaiser's measure of sampling adequacy in this analysis was .938. Using a .40 cutoff, the result initially showed an eleven-factor structure that is the same as the English version. These eleven factors explained 65 percent of total variance. However, one of the factors had only two items with loading greater than .40, which was too weak to be considered as a factor, so it was dropped. A new factor emerged that merged items associated with the Transfer Design and

Opportunity to Use Learning constructs in the original LTSI. The new factor was labeled Transferability and defined as the extent to which trainees perceive that training is designed to facilitate opportunity to apply what they learn to the job. Twelve items were deleted in terms of problems with low loadings, serious cross-loadings, and noninterpretable factors: items 1, 17, 25, 27, 44, 50, 51, 52, 60, 61, 62, and 63. The factor analysis results are in Table 3.

In the Training in General domain, twenty-six items were used. These items included twenty-three validated items and three research items. The ratio of respondents to items in this analysis was 22.2 to 1. Kaiser's measure of sampling adequacy in this analysis was .933. The results showed a five-factor structure and were consistent with the original LTSI factors. The five factors explained 61.4 percent of the total variance. All items were retained with exception of the item 64, which was eliminated because of low loading. The factor analysis results are in Table 4.

Overall, in the eighty-nine-item factor analysis, either the six problematic factors reemerged or had reliabilities improved. The exceptions were the Opportunity to Use Learning and Transfer Design factors, which combined into the Transferability scale in Taiwan's settings. Seventy-six items were retained. In terms of the result of this research question, the scale definitions of the LTSI were redefined to fit Taiwan's settings. The TLTSI scale definitions, sample items, number of items and reliability for each scale are in Table 5.

**Research Question 3.** Additional factor analyses were conducted to compare the factor structures with and without the respondents who attended affective-related training, which was the spiritual inspiration training course. Ninety-nine responses were collected from the training. Because an appropriate sample size for a factor analysis is to have responses to items ratios from 5 to 1 to 10 to 1 (Hair et al., 1998), ideally we would like to have had more data from the affective training so the responses could be factor-analyzed separately. However, this was not possible in this data set. An alternative was to exclude the responses from the affective training in factor analyses. If the responses of the affective-related training did not fit the instrument, the factor structures between the data set with and without the affective training should show substantial differences. The result is shown in Table 6. In comparing the result of this research question to research questions 1 and 2, the factor structures do not differ substantially between the data sets with and without the affective-related training.

**Research Question 4.** Analyses for research questions 1 and 2 indicated that this study was able to validate comparable transfer factors for a cross-cultural study between Taiwan and the United States. In terms of the results of the research question 1, eleven transfer factors are comparable. The results of research question 2 suggested that fourteen of the validated factors in this study were identical to the original LTSI. It is possible that an updated validation study of the English version of the LTSI with the research items will

## Table 3. Rotated Factor Loadings for Training in Specific Domain of the Sixty-Three-Item Analysis

| Item | Factor | | | | | | | | | | | Communality ($R^2$) |
| | 1 | 2 | 3 | 4 | 5 | 6 | 7 | 8 | 9 | 10 | 11 | |
|---|---|---|---|---|---|---|---|---|---|---|---|---|
| Q58 | .62 | | | | | | | | .22 | | | .74 |
| Q55 | .56 | | | | | | | | | | | .66 |
| Q59 | .52 | | | | | | | | .21 | | | .61 |
| Q54 | .50 | | | | | | | | .23 | | | .63 |
| Q56 | .48 | | | | | | | | | | | .62 |
| Q53 | .45 | | | | | | | | .24 | | | .58 |
| Q57 | .40 | | | | | | | | | | | .65 |
| Q60 | .37 | | | | | | | | | | | .51 |
| Q35 | | .84 | | | | | | | | | | .71 |
| Q34 | | .82 | | | | | | | | | | .68 |
| Q36 | | .77 | | | | | | | | | | .72 |
| Q38 | | .75 | | | | | | | | | | .57 |
| Q41 | | .72 | | | | | | | | | | .67 |
| Q42 | | .69 | | | | | | | | | | .57 |
| Q45 | | .64 | | | | | | | | | | .60 |
| Q46 | | .58 | | | | | | | | | | .44 |
| Q8 | | | -.87 | | | | | | | | | .72 |
| Q6 | | | -.83 | | | | | | | | | .74 |
| Q7 | | | -.79 | | | | | | | | | .69 |
| Q22 | | | -.76 | | | | | | | | | .70 |
| Q16 | | | -.72 | | | | | | | | | .67 |
| Q18 | | -.20 | -.48 | | | | | | | | | .51 |
| Q17 | | | -.45 | | | | | | | | | .57 |
| Q15 | | | -.41 | -.36 | | | | | | | | .45 |

*(Continued)*

## Table 3. Rotated Factor Loadings for Training in Specific Domain of the Sixty-Three-Item Analysis (Continued)

| Item | | | | | | | Factor | | | | | Communality ($R^2$) |
|------|---|---|---|---|---|---|---|---|---|---|---|---|
| | 1 | 2 | 3 | 4 | 5 | 6 | 7 | 8 | 9 | 10 | 11 | |
| Q23 | | | | -.80 | | | | | | | | .65 |
| Q21 | | | | -.73 | | | | | | | | .63 |
| Q14 | | | | -.57 | | | | | | | | .50 |
| Q24 | | | | -.55 | | | | | | | | .50 |
| Q39 | | | | | -.79 | | | | | | | .69 |
| Q40 | | | | | -.74 | | | | | | | .68 |
| Q33 | | | | | -.73 | | | | | | | .74 |
| Q37 | | | | | -.72 | | | | | | | .65 |
| Q43 | | | | | -.67 | | | | | | | .60 |
| Q32 | | | | | -.66 | | | | | | | .69 |
| Q44 | | | | | -.39 | | | | | | | .28 |
| Q62 | .23 | | | | -.26 | .23 | | | | | | .32 |
| Q30 | | | | | | .84 | | | | | | .78 |
| Q29 | | | | | | .79 | | | | | | .75 |
| Q28 | | | | | | .69 | | | | | | .62 |
| Q31 | | | | | | .60 | | | | | | .58 |
| Q4 | | | | | | | -.67 | | | | | .63 |
| Q5 | | | | | | | -.63 | | | | | .55 |
| Q3 | | | | | | | -.61 | | | | | .58 |
| Q2 | | | | | | | -.55 | | | | | .52 |
| Q1 | | | | | | | -.37 | | | .33 | | .41 |

|  |  |  |  |  |  |  |  |  |  |  |  |  |
|---|---|---|---|---|---|---|---|---|---|---|---|---|
| Q20 |  |  |  |  |  |  |  | .63 |  |  |  | .51 |
| Q11 |  |  |  |  |  |  |  | .61 |  |  |  | .56 |
| Q12 |  |  |  |  |  |  |  | .56 |  |  |  | .48 |
| Q26 |  |  |  |  |  |  |  | .46 |  |  |  | .37 |
| Q19 |  |  |  |  |  |  |  | −.44 |  |  |  | .44 |
| Q61 |  |  |  |  |  |  |  | .33 |  |  |  | .24 |
| Q25 |  |  |  |  | −.21 |  |  | −.25 |  |  |  | .35 |
| Q48 |  |  |  |  |  |  |  |  | .80 |  |  | .78 |
| Q47 |  |  |  |  |  |  |  |  | .75 |  |  | .65 |
| Q49 | .30 |  |  |  |  |  |  |  | .47 |  |  | .67 |
| Q50 | .32 |  |  |  |  |  |  |  | .32 |  | .30 | .69 |
| Q10 |  |  |  |  |  |  |  |  |  | .63 |  | .45 |
| Q13 |  |  |  |  |  |  |  |  |  | .55 |  | .33 |
| Q9 |  |  |  |  |  |  | −.26 | .23 |  | .41 |  | .50 |
| Q63 |  |  |  |  |  |  |  |  |  | .24 |  | .26 |
| Q52 | .34 |  |  |  |  |  |  |  | .27 |  | .41 | .71 |
| Q51 | .21 |  |  |  |  |  |  |  | .33 |  | .41 | .71 |
| Q27 |  |  |  |  |  |  |  |  |  |  | .29 | .24 |
| Eigenvalues | 17.82 | 6.92 | 3.73 | 2.18 | 2.03 | 1.77 | 1.65 | 1.52 | 1.21 | 1.09 | 1.04 |  |
| Percentage of variance | 28.29 | 10.98 | 5.93 | 3.46 | 3.22 | 2.81 | 2.61 | 2.41 | 1.92 | 1.73 | 1.66 |  |

Note: Cross-loadings less than .20 are not listed.

**Table 4. Rotated Factor Loadings for Training in General Domain of the Twenty-Six-Item Analysis**

| Item | 1 | 2 | 3 | 4 | 5 | Communality ($R^2$) |
|------|-----|-----|-----|-----|-----|-----|
| | | | *Factor* | | | |
| Q68 | .67 | | | | | .63 |
| Q67 | .65 | | | | | .39 |
| Q70 | .59 | | | | | .50 |
| Q72 | .49 | | | | | .44 |
| Q79 | .45 | | | .25 | | .41 |
| Q64 | −.23 | .23 | | | | .18 |
| Q77 | | .78 | | | | .60 |
| Q76 | | .72 | | | | .57 |
| Q74 | | .65 | | | | .43 |
| Q73 | | .62 | | | | .37 |
| Q75 | | −.42 | | | | .35 |
| Q78 | .29 | −.40 | | | | .43 |
| Q84 | | | −.82 | | | .67 |
| Q85 | | | −.77 | | | .64 |
| Q83 | | | −.77 | | | .57 |
| Q82 | | | −.62 | | | .64 |
| Q86 | | | | .80 | | .69 |
| Q81 | | | | .80 | | .67 |
| Q80 | | | | .79 | | .68 |
| Q88 | .25 | | | .60 | | .65 |
| Q89 | | | −.26 | .45 | | .36 |
| Q87 | | | | .43 | | .46 |
| Q66 | | | | | −.67 | .65 |
| Q71 | | | | | −.60 | .63 |
| Q69 | .28 | | | | −.58 | .66 |
| Q65 | | | −.24 | | −.46 | .50 |
| Eigenvalues | 9.35 | 2.37 | 1.76 | 1.49 | 1.00 | |
| Percentage of variance | 36.00 | 9.11 | 6.75 | 5.71 | 3.86 | |

*Note:* Cross-loadings less than .20 are not listed.

provide more factors that are comparable, statistically reliable, and valid between these two countries. It is important to note that although the items retained in the validated factors in research questions 1 and 2 were not completely identical to the items in the original LTSI, one way to provide coherent comparisons is to select items that are valid in both the original LTSI and TLTSI. However, this must be justified by acceptable reliabilities and adjustments in definition of the factors. A comparison table between the LTSI and the TLTSI can be found in Table 6.

**Table 5. TLTSI Scale Definitions and Sample Items**

| Factor | Definition | Sample Item | Number of Item | α |
|---|---|---|---|---|
| Trainee characteristics factors | | | | |
| Learner Readiness | The extent to which an individual knows expected outcomes of the training and understands how the training are prepared for them prior to participating in training. | Before the training I had a good understanding of how it would fit my job-related development. | 3 | .65 |
| Performance Self-Efficacy | The extent to which an individual's belief in self on overcoming obstacles to change his or her performance. | I am confident in my ability to use newly learned skills on the job. | 4 | .86 |
| Motivation factors | | | | |
| Motivation to Transfer | The extent to which an individual's willingness and excitement to try out new learning to the job and belief in new skills will help him or her improve job performance. | I get excited when I think about trying to use my new learning on the job. | 4 | .83 |
| Transfer Effort– Performance Expectations | The extent to which an individual's belief and expectation in effort will lead to performance improvement. | My job performance improves when I use new things that I have learned. | 4 | .85 |
| Performance- Outcomes Expectations | The extent to which an individual expect that changes in job performance will lead to valued outcomes. | For the most part, the people who get rewarded around here are the ones that do something to deserve it. | 5 | .80 |
| Work environment factors | | | | |
| Positive Personal Outcomes | The extent to which applying training on the job leads to outcomes, which are positive for the individual. The positive outcomes may include pay raise, incentives, non-momentary rewards, and public recognition. | If I use this training I am more likely to be rewarded. | 7 | .91 |

*(Continued)*

**Table 5. TLTSI Scale Definitions and Sample Items (Continued)**

| Factor | Definition | Sample Item | Number of Item | α |
|---|---|---|---|---|
| Negative Personal Outcomes | The extent to which an individual believes that *not* applying skills and knowledge learned in training will lead to outcomes that are negative. The negative outcomes may be oral warning, tangible penalty, notification, and some type of punishment. | If I do not utilize my training I will be cautioned about it. | 4 | .79 |
| Peer Support | The extent to which an individual's peers reinforce and support use of learning on the job. The reinforcement and support may include a peer's appreciation, encouragement, expectation, and patience to the individual's efforts in transferring learned knowledge and skills to his or her job. | My colleagues encourage me to use the skills I have learned in training. | 4 | .89 |
| Supervisor Support | The extent to which an individual's supervisors or managers reinforce and support use of training on the job. The reinforcement and support may include supervisor or manager accessibility, addressing concerns on a regular basis, demonstration of interest about work problems, and facilitation of achievable goal setting for the individual in relation to transfer issues. | My supervisor helps me set realistic goals for job performance based on my training. | 6 | .92 |

| | Description | Sample Item | | |
|---|---|---|---|---|
| Supervisor Sanctions | The extent to which an individual perceives negative responses and actions from his or her supervisors or managers as applying skills and knowledge learned in training. Negative responses and actions may include objection, negatively tacit cues, lack of interests, and critiques in relation to transfer issues. | My supervisor thinks I am being less effective when I use the techniques taught in this training. | 8 | .92 |
| Openness to Change (reversal code) | The extent to which an individual perceives that group norms are to resist or discourage the application of skills and knowledge learned in training. | Experienced employees in my group ridicule others when they use techniques they learn in training. | 6 | .80 |
| Transferability | The extent to which an individual perceives that training is designed to facilitate opportunities to apply what they learn to the job. Opportunities may include resource availability in the job and case examples and participation in the training. | The way the trainer(s) taught the material made me feel more confident I could apply it. | 7 | .92 |
| Ability factors | | | | |
| Personal Capacity for Transfer | The extent to which an individual has the time, energy and mental space in their job to transfer learned skills and knowledge to the job. | My workload allows me time to try the new things I have learned. | 5 | .78 |
| Perceived Content Validity | The extent to which an individual judges the match between training content and job requirements. | The methods used in training are very similar to how we do it on the job. | 3 | .84 |
| Performance Coaching | Formal and informal indicators from an organization about an individual's job performance. The indicators may include advice, suggestions, feedback, and conversation from others. | After training, I get feedback from people about how well I am applying what I learned. | 6 | .88 |

**Table 6. Factors, Reliabilities, and Items Comparisons of the Extended Analyses Between LTSI and TLTSI**

| Training in Specific | LTSI (eleven factors) Validated Items | Research Items | Results of Research Question 1 TLTSI (seven factors) Items | Results of Research Question 2 TLTSI (ten factors) Items | Results of Research Question 3 Forty-Five-Item Analysis (seven factors) Items | Sixty-Three-Item Analysis (nine factors) Items | Results of Research Question 4 |
|---|---|---|---|---|---|---|---|
| Learner Readiness | 1, 9, 10, 13 (.73) | | 1, 9, 10, 13 (.73) | 9, 10, 13 (.65) | 9, 10, 13 | 1, 2, 3, 4, 9, 10, 13 | C |
| Motivation to Transfer | 2, 3, 4, 5 (.83) | | 2, 3, 4, 5 (.83) | 2, 3, 4, 5 (.83) | 2, 3, 4, 5 | | C |
| Positive Personal Outcomes | 6, 16, 17 (.69) | 7, 8, 15, 18, 22 | 6, 16, 17 (.69) | 6, 7, 8, 15, 16, 18, 22 (.91) | 6, 16, 17 | 6, 7, 8, 15, 16, 17, 22 | C |
| Negative Personal Outcomes | 14, 21, 23, 24 (.76) | | 14, 21, 23, 24 (.79) | 14, 21, 23, 24 (.79) | 14, 21, 23, 24 | 14, 21, 23, 24 | C |
| Personal Capacity for Transfer | 19, 25, **26,** 27 (.68) | 11, 12, 20 | | **11, 12,** 19, **20, 26** (.78) | | **11, 12, 20, 26** | PC |
| Peer Support | 28, 29, 30, 31 (.83) | | 28, 29, 30, 31 (.89) | 28, 29, 30, 31 (.89) | 28, 29, 30, 31 | 28, 29, 30, 31 | C |
| Supervisor Support | 32, 33, 37, 39, 40, 43 (.91) | | 32, 33, 37, 39, 40, 43, 44 (.89) | 32, 33, 37, 39, 40, 43 (.92) | 32, 33, 37, 39, 40, 43, 44 | 32, 33, 37, 39, 40, 43 | C |
| Supervisor Sanction | 38, 44, 45 (.63) | 34, 35, 36, 41, 42, 46 | 38, 45 (.69)[a] | 34, 35, 36, 38, 41, 42, 45, 46 (.92) | 38, 45 | 34, 35, 36, 38, 41, 42, 45 | PC |

| _Training in General_ | _LTSI_ (five factors) | _TLTSI_ (four factors) | _TLTSI_ (five factors) | _TLTSI_ (five factors) | _Twenty-Three-Item Analysis_ (four factors) | _Twenty-Six-Item Analysis_ (five factors) | |
|---|---|---|---|---|---|---|---|
| Perceived Content Validity | 47, 48, 49, 58, 59 (.84) | | | 47, 48, 49 (.84) | 47, 48, 49, 52, 53, 54, 55, 56, 58, 59, 60 | 47, 48, 49 | C |
| Transfer Design | 52, 53, 54, 55 (.85) | | | 53, 54, 55, 56, 57, 58, 59 (.92)- labeled as Transferability | 53, 54, 55, 56, 58, 59, 60 | 50, 51, 52, 54, 55, 56, 57 | |
| Opportunity to Use Learning | 56, 60, **61**, **63** (.7) | 50, 51, 57, 62 | 61 (n/a) | | 61, 63[a] | | |
| Transfer Effort-Performance Expectation | 65, 66, 69, 71 (.81) | | 65, 66, 69, 71 (.83) | 65, 66, 69, 71 (.85) | 66, 69, 71 | 65, 66, 69, 71 | C |
| Performance-Outcome Expectation | **64**, 67, 68, 70, 72 (.83) | | 67, 68, 70, 72, 79 (.80) | 67, 68, 70, 72, 79 (.80) | 67, 68, 70, 72, 79 | 67, 68, 70, 72, 79 | C |
| Openness to Change | 73, 74, **75**, 76, 77, **78** (.85) | | **73**, **74**, 75, **76**, **77**, 78 (.80) | **73**, **74**, 75, **76**, **77**, 78 (.80) | 73, 74, 75, **76**, **77**, 78 | 73, 74, 75, **76**, **77**, 78 | C |
| Performance Self-Efficacy | 82, 83, 84, 85 (.76) | | 82, 83, 84, 85, 89 (.84) | 82, 83, 84, 85 (.86) | 82, 83, 84, 85, 89 | 82, 83, 84, 85 | C |
| Performance Coaching | 79, 86, 87, 89 (.7) | 80, 81, 88 | | 80, 81, 86, 87, 88, 89 (.88) | | 80, 81, 86, 87, 88, 89 | PC |

_Note:_ The numbers in the parentheses represent reliability. Factor extraction was based on a .40 cutoff criterion for all analyses. Bold numbers represent reverse-scored items.

[a]A valid factor has more than two items. C = comparable factor; PC = potentially comparable factor.

## Conclusion and Discussion

Most of the cross-cultural research that translates instruments from one language to another has been based on direct translation methods, and many of the translation processes are completed based solely on a researcher's satisfaction (Sperber et al., 1994). This study undertook a more rigorous translation process by using the forward-back translation approach with subjective, objective, and pilot evaluations of the translation that goes beyond what many cross-cultural studies do and what most of the cross-cultural research in HRD has done. The rigorous translation process has enhanced the quality of this research endeavor and reduced the biases that likely would have occurred in the translation process.

Through the rigorous translation and evaluation process, the result of research question 1 suggested that eleven factors of the LTSI are validated in Taiwan's organizations. When the research items were included in another analysis, the result of research question 2 indicated that the valid factors grew to fifteen and the reliabilities of the problematic factors were all improved with only one exception, Opportunity to Use Learning, which was factor-analyzed as part of the new factor, Transferability. The finding of research question 2 indicated that the seventy-six factor-analyzed items are more appropriate for use in Taiwan than items in research question 1 because they provide stronger validity and reliability in Taiwanese organizations. The results of research question 3 indicated that LTSI can be used for affective-related training. In terms of analysis of research question 4, eleven validated factors in research question 1 appear to be comparable between the LTSI and TLTSI. However, the result also implies that a validation study in U.S. organizations including the research items may provide more comparable factors between the LTSI and TLTSI. Such a study is being conducted by the LTSI authors.

The differences in the instrument items and factor structures between Taiwan and the United States can be looked at from four perspectives: cultural, instrument design, translation, and implementation. First, the five factors of the original LTSI—Personal Capacity for Transfer, Supervisor Sanction, Transfer Design, Opportunity to Use Learning, and Performance Coaching—that were not validated in research question 1 could be due to cultural variation. However, the results of research question 2 suggested that three of these LTSI factors (Personal Capacity for Transfer, Supervisor Sanction, and Performance Coaching) were different in initial analyses due to issues of instrument design. Specifically, the low reliabilities in these three factors in the original LTSI suggested problematic items in English, which were magnified when translated into Chinese. The fact that including the stronger research items from the original LTSI eliminated the differences demonstrates that cultural differences were not the explanation.

Thus, the only difference that occurs between Taiwan and the United States is the merger of two original LTSI factors, Transfer Design and Opportunity to

Use Learning. This cultural variation could be explained by variations in training delivery method. The predominant training delivery method in Taiwan is more lecture oriented. Relatively few training courses are designed in ways to encourage participation and involvement. In this sense, the concept of Transfer Design in the United States, which encourages participation and involvement, might not be perceived as a unique factor in Taiwan's culture. Instead, trainees in Taiwan may perceive Transfer Design and Opportunity to Use Learning as a single construct of Transferability. Specifically, trainees in Taiwan may perceive training that they will have an opportunity to use as constituting a good transfer design.

However, there was one important difference in the implementation of this study that could also have caused the factor structure to vary in this way. Specifically, the data were collected at the end of one or two weeks after training in this study. In contrast, the data for the original LTSI were all collected at the end (Holton et al., 2000). The differences in implementation between these two studies could have influenced the factor structures. For example, respondents who returned the instruments two weeks after training may have perceived Opportunity to Use Learning and Transfer Design as one concept, because at the two-week point, they would know whether they had been able to use their training. Those who completed the instrument at the end of training may have been able to differentiate between the two constructs. These people would have reflected on the concept of Opportunity to Use Learning based on their perceptions of what they believed would happen in their work settings, while the latter respondents would have actually experienced whether they could apply the training to their jobs. Thus, it is possible that the concepts of Transfer Design and Opportunity to Use Learning may be indistinguishable to participants two weeks after training. In addition, their recall of course activities would be biased by their experience on the job. The first author attempted to separate these two groups and examine the factor structure for each group. Unfortunately, records were not kept of which surveys were returned after two weeks after training, so the analysis could not be completed. However, it is believed that enough were returned after training to possibly have altered the factor structure.

The differences in the factor structures could also be due to translation errors. However, it is reasonable to think that the translation errors had been controlled because of the extensive translation procedures conducted. The subjective evaluation that was examined by the original author enhanced the precision of the translation because the author is the most qualified individual to know what the factors were intended to be measured in the instrument. The third-party persons who objectively evaluated the translation helped minimize both the author's and the researcher's bias. In addition, the pilot test with a group of Taiwanese individuals also helped ensure that the translation used common language in Taiwan so the readability of the instrument was enhanced. All of these efforts led to a reduction of translation errors and increased the functional equivalence between the instruments in two languages.

*Implications for HRD Research and Practice.* This study successfully validated a transfer instrument for use in Taiwan and provides opportunities to compare transfer systems between Taiwan and U.S. organizations. The validated instrument is also valuable to HRD research and practice. From a research perspective, the successful validation has increased the generalizability of the LTSI in two ways. First, using the Taiwanese sample in this study expands the application of the LTSI to Taiwan and extends the cross-cultural validity of the LTSI. Second, the findings of research question 3 also suggest that the LTSI could be used in affective-related training.

Moreover, synthesizing findings of research questions 1, 2, and 4, the results point to some possible revisions in the original LTSI (the instrument authors are working on a revised version). This study found that the five low-reliability factors in the original LTSI are somewhat associated with the factors that did not emerge or continued to have reliability problems. The same evidence can be found in Yamnill (2001). This implied that the twenty-one research items are well-developed items that would improve the reliability of the instrument, and further investigation of the twenty-one research items needs to be done in English to test this assumption.

With regard to implications for practice, Taiwan's government and organizations highly value the importance of training but have not be able to respond appropriately to transfer issues. This study makes a timely contribution to HRD practice in Taiwan because it provides a valid, statistically reliable, culturally appropriate, and comprehensive instrument to organizations in Taiwan for diagnosing the strengths and weaknesses of the transfer systems. Accurate diagnosis of problems of transfer systems also creates opportunities for performance improvement. Organizations in Taiwan should shift the focus of training evaluation to higher levels (to transfer and results, for example) so training budgets can be effectively deployed. In an aggregated view, improvement of individual performance will lead to improved organizational performance and ultimately contribute to the nation's economic growth. In addition, for cross-cultural HRD practice, as globalization evolves, international business will require more and more cross-cultural training for employees. This study provides comparable measures of transfer systems that will enable organizations to cross-culturally assess transfer issues for performance improvement and avoid an ethnocentric focus.

*Limitations.* We acknowledge that an assumption of fully translatable languages is the major limitation of this study even if the evaluations of translation were conducted. Indeed, this assumption highlights the limitation of the forward-back translation process. Since the two languages are so different, some translation dilemmas occurred. For example, the word *perk* used in the original LTSI was translated as "nonmonetary reward." However, some problems with word choice could only be minimized and were not completely solved. For example, the words *punishment, penalty,* and *reprimand* in the original LTSI represent three different degrees of negative consequences in English. However, to differentiate these three words clearly in Mandarin would have required more than one sentence of explanation, which was not suitable for a questionnaire. The dilemma was that if the author did not completely capture the differences among the three words in translation, then the participants' responses on the TLTSI might differ from those of the original LTSI. If the author fully captured the differences of the three words, then the items in the TLTSI might be awkward in reading because of the long sentences. Other examples such as language structure (for example, Mandarin has no tense or plural form) could also have affected the results.

One alternative in cross-cultural instrument development is to use a simultaneous instrument development approach. That is, researchers can first generate constructs of interests from both cultures. Once the constructs are identified and determined, they can then develop instruments for each language so that language limitations are eliminated. Although this approach has great potential to eliminate language issues, it also raises issues of cross-cultural comparability of results.

Self-report data, nonrandom sampling, and other types of training and organizations that were not included in this study are other limitations. However, through the purposive sampling technique, we believe that the sample collected from this study reached a level of heterogeneity that its generalizability is vastly improved over construct validation studies collecting data from a single organization, school, or training. This is supported by the characteristics of subjects collected from five different organizational types (public, private, educational, nonprofit, and public-for-profit organizations) and various training types (skill-based, knowledge-based, and affective-related training) in this study.

**Future Research Directions.** This study has provided an initial attempt to develop a valid transfer instrument in Taiwan by validating the LTSI. However, the development of such an instrument is not complete yet. Future research should focus on investigating the relatively low reliability scales (Learner Readiness) and the possible effect of the time delay in collecting some data, which may have led to identifying the new factor (Transferability) in the validated TLTSI. Additional factors such as personality (Tziner, Haccoun, & Kadish, 1991), relapse prevention (Burke, 1997), and culturally specific factors in Taiwan's literature and practice that have not been included in the TLTSI should also be reviewed and examined.

Additional data should be collected from affective-related training. Although the approach used in this study provides reasonable evidence that the TLTSI fits affective-related training, further research to confirm this finding with a larger sample including other affective-related training, such as emotional intelligence, would seem to be important.

Other research directions include attempting to confirm the factor structure by using confirmatory factor analysis with different samples, reducing the size of the instrument to keep it parsimonious while retaining the factor structure and its psychometric quality, and using the TLTSI to examine transfer systems across organizations in Taiwan. A parsimonious transfer instrument will benefit Taiwan's HRD practice in two ways. It will be even more culturally appropriate because individuals tend to be reluctant to complete a long survey due to the effect of overused subjects in Taiwan. It is also more desirable for HRD professionals because the time used by the employees to complete the questionnaire is an opportunity cost of training budgets in many organizations. A more parsimonious instrument would also facilitate studies to compare transfer systems across organizations in Taiwan and establish the criterion validity of the TLTSI.

Future research in validation of the LTSI to other countries should use both validated and research items so the factors that may exist would not be inappropriately eliminated. Finally, since this study has established some comparable transfer factors, future research should conduct comparative studies between transfer systems in Taiwan and the United States.

## References

Ary, D., Jacobs, L. C., & Razavieh, A. (1996). *Introduction to research in education.* (5th ed.). Fort Worth, TX: Harcourt Brace.

Baldwin, T. T., & Ford, K. J. (1988). Transfer of training: A review and directions for future research. *Personnel Psychology, 41,* 63–105.

Bates, R. A., & Holton, E. F. III. (2004). Linking workplace literacy skills and transfer system perceptions. *Human Resource Development Quarterly, 15,* 153–170.

Bates, R. A., Holton, E. F. III, & Seyler, D. L. (1997). Factors affecting transfer of training in an industrial setting. In R. Torraco (Ed.), *Proceedings of the Academy of Human Resource Development Annual Conference Proceedings, USA* (pp. 345–359). Bowling Green, OH: Academy of Human Resource Development.

Bates, R. A., Holton, E. F. III, Seyler, D. L., & Carvalho, M. B. (2000). The role of interpersonal factors in the application of computer-based training in an industrial setting. *Human Resource Development International, 3,* 19–42.

Bookter, A. I. (1999). *Convergent and divergent validity of the learning transfer questionnaire.* Unpublished doctoral dissertation, Louisiana State University.

Brislin, R. W. (1970). Back-translation for cross-cultural research. *Cross-Cultural Psychology, 1,* 185–216.

Bullinger, M., Anderson, R., Cella, D., & Aronson, N. (1993). Developing and evaluating cross-cultural instruments from minimum requirements to optimal models. *Quality of Life Research, 2,* 451–459.

Burke, L. A. (1997). Improving positive transfer: A test of relapse prevention training on transfer outcomes. *Human Resource Development Quarterly, 8,* 115–126.

Chen, H.-C. (2003). *Cross-cultural construct validation of Learning Transfer System Inventory in Taiwan.* Unpublished doctoral dissertation, Louisiana State University.

Chen, Y.-H. (1997). *A study of the influences of the work environment and trainee characteristics on the transfer of training.* Unpublished master's thesis, National Chaio Tung University, Hsinchu, Taiwan. [in Chinese]

Chuang, T.-H. (1998, June 5). Economic perspectives of entrepreneurs. *Common Wealth,* 52–58.

Chuo, Y.-C. (1997). *The relation between organization factors and the transfer of training in life-insurance industry.* Unpublished master's thesis, National Chung Hsing University, Taichung, Taiwan. [in Chinese]

Civil Servant Life-Long Learning Act. (2002). Taipei, Taiwan: Legislative Yuan. [http://law.moj.gov.tw].

Cornelius, P. K. (2003). *The global competitiveness report 2002–2003: World Economic Forum.* New York: Oxford University Press.

Ford, J. K., & Weissbein, D. A. (1997). Transfer of training: An update review and analysis. *Performance Improvement Quarterly, 10,* 22–41.

Hair, J. F., Anderson, R. E., Tatham, R. L., & Black, W. C. (1998). *Multivariate data analysis* (5th ed.). Englewood Cliffs, NJ: Prentice Hall.

Hendriks, A.A.J., Perugini, M., Angleitner, A., Ostendorf, F., De Fruyt, F., Hrebickova, M., Hebíková, M., Kreitler, S., Murakami, T., Bratko, D., Conner, M., Nagy, J., Rodríguez-Fornells, A., & Ruisel, I. (2003). The five-factor personality inventory: Cross-cultural generalizability across 13 countries. *European Journal of Personality, 17,* 347–373.

Hofstede, G. (2001). *Culture's consequences: Comparing values, behaviors, institutions, and organizations across nations* (2nd ed.). Thousand Oaks, CA: Sage.

Holton, E. F. III. (1996). The flawed four-level evaluation model. *Human Resource Development Quarterly, 7,* 5–21.

Holton, E. F. III, Bates, R. A., & Ruona, W. E. (2000). Development of a generalized learning transfer system inventory. *Human Resource Development Quarterly, 11,* 333–360.

Holton, E. F., III., Bates, R. A., Seyler, D. L., & Carvalho, M. B. (1997). Toward construct validation of a transfer climate instrument. *Human Resource Development Quarterly, 8,* 95–113.

Holton, E. F. III., Chen, H.-C., & Naquin, S. S. (2003). An examination of learning transfer system characteristics across organizational settings. *Human Resource Development Quarterly, 14,* 459–482.

Hui, C. H., & Triandis, H. C. (1985). Measurement in cross-cultural psychology: A review and comparison of strategies. *Journal of Cross-Cultural Psychology, 16,* 131–152.

Jackson, T. (2001). Cultural values and management ethics: A 10 nation study. *Human Relation, 54,* 1267–1302.

Kabanoff, B., & Bottger, P. (1991). Effectiveness of creativity training and its relation to selected personality factors. *Journal of Organizational Behavior, 12,* 235–248.

Kraiger, K., Ford, J. K., & Salas, E. (1993). Application of cognitive, skill-based, and affective theories of learning outcomes to new methods of training evaluation. *Journal of Applied Psychology, 78,* 311–328.

Kuo, C. M., & McLean, G. N. (1999). The history of human resource development in Taiwan from 1949 to 1999. In K. P. Kuchinke (Ed.), *Academy of Human Resource Development Conference Proceeding, USA* (p. 15–1). Bowling Green, OH: Academy of Human Resource Development.

Lin, Y.-Y., & Chiu, H.-Y. (1997). The evaluation of training and development: An empirical study. *Journal of Human Resource Development, 7,* 67–83. [in Chinese]

Noe, R. A. (1986). Trainee attributes and attitudes: Neglected influences on training effectiveness. *Academy of Management Review, 11,* 736–749.

Noe, R. A., & Schmitt, N. (1986). The influence of trainee attitudes on training effectiveness: Test of a model. *Personnel Psychology, 39,* 497–523.

Nunnally, J. C., & Bernstein, J. H. (1994). *Psychometric theory* (3rd ed.). New York: McGraw-Hill.

Ruona, W.E.A., Leimbach, M., Holton, E. F. III., & Bates, R. A. (2002). The relationship between learner utility reactions and predictors of learning transfer among trainees. *International Journal of Training and Development, 6,* 218–228.

Schwab, K. (2004). *The global competitiveness report 2003–2004: World Economic Forum.* New York: Oxford University Press.

Seyler, D. L., Holton, E. F. III., Bates, R. A., Burnett, M. F., & Carvalho, M. B. (1998). Factors affecting motivation to transfer training. *International Journal of Training and Development, 2,* 2–16.

Sperber, A. D., Devellis, R. F., & Boehlecke, B. (1994). Cross-cultural translation: Methodology and validation. *Journal of Cross-Cultural Psychology, 25,* 501–524.

Steiner, D. D., Dobbins, G. H., & Trahan, W. A. (1991). The trainer-trainee interaction: An attributional model of training. *Journal of Organizational Behavior, 12*, 271–286.

Tabachnick, B. G., & Fidell, L. S. (1996). *Using multivariate statistics* (3rd ed.). New York: HarperCollins.

Tziner, A. Haccoun, R. R., & Kadish, A. (1991). Personal and situational characteristics influencing the effectiveness of transfer of training improvement strategies. *Journal of Occupational Psychology, 64*, 167–177.

Yamnill, S. (2001). *Factors affecting transfer of training in Thailand.* Unpublished doctoral dissertation, University of Minnesota.

Yuen, S.-C. (1994). Vocational and technical education: An important player in Taiwan's economic success. *Occupational Education Forum, 22*, 2–21.

*Hsin-Chih Chen is a postdoctoral research associate in human resource, leadership, and workforce development at Louisiana State University.*

*E. F. Holton III is professor in human resource and leadership development at Louisiana State University.*

*Reid Bates is associate professor in human resource and leadership development at Louisiana State University.*

For bulk reprints of this article, please call (201) 748-8789.

# Work Design Theory: A Review and Critique with Implications for Human Resource Development

*Richard J. Torraco*

*Six theoretical perspectives on work design are examined for their contributions to our understanding of how work is organized and designed in organizations: sociotechnical systems theory, process improvement, adaptive structuration theory, the job characteristics model, technostructural change models, and activity theory. A critique of these theories raises concerns about their ability to explain the design of work in new work environments. The critique highlights the need to eliminate the discontinuity in how theory explains the structure and articulation of work among system levels. The implications of this study for further research on work design theory and for human resource development practice are discussed.*

Work design is tightly woven into the structure and function of organizations. The nature of work and how it is structured and related to human activity affects every aspect of the organization. Work design is the basis for how work is conceived in broad terms, translated across organizational levels, and structured for the units and the individuals who perform the work. The structure, technology, and resources available in one's work environment are fundamental to the meaning and value one places in work. As such, the organization and design of one's work environment significantly shape the contribution one makes to the organization.

The nature of work continues to change (Howard, 1995; Cappelli, Bassi, Katz, Knoke, Osterman, & Useem, 1997), and the rate of change in work design and technology continues to accelerate (Adler, 1992; Tenner, 1996). With the instant availability of information and reduced geographical distances (Schick, Gordon, & Haka, 1990), today's work processes are fundamentally different from those routinely used just a decade ago (Barley & Orr, 1997; Luff, Hindmarsh, & Heath, 2000; Norman, 1998). New work requirements have brought about major changes in how work is designed (Parker & Wall, 1998) and accomplished (Osterman, 1994). This raises important questions about the adequacy of our understanding of work and work design. Has work design theory kept up with the reality of practice? Do the theories we rely on to explain how work is organized accurately reflect today's fluid work environments? An important development in work design is the increasing opportunity for virtual work and the emergence of alternative locations for work (Apgar, 1998). How well do existing theories explain work design in virtual and other nontraditional work environments? Have the realities of practice outstripped the capacity of theory to provide an adequate understanding of these issues? The problem addressed by this article is that many features of emerging work designs are not adequately explained by existing work design theories, which means that managers, human resource development (HRD) professionals, and others may be relying on outdated models for making decisions about work design, job requirements, and the employee skills needed to meet these requirements.

This article paper reviews and critiques existing work design theories and then uses this critique, to stimulate new ways of thinking about work design that explain more effectively the challenges and opportunities for employees in today's workplace. HRD professionals are concerned about work design because those who are responsible for employee development cannot afford to lose sight of these recent developments in work design since many new skills in need of development emerge from changes in work requirements and work design. John P. Campbell and colleagues reminded us of the importance of linking training design with work design: "Training contents do not just fall out of some big training bin in the sky" (Campbell, McCloy, Oppler, & Sager, 1993, p. 38). The nature and design of the work itself will always be an important determinant of the composition of employee skills needed to perform the work.

As the basis for a critique of how well existing work design theories explain the realities of today's workplace, this article reviews six theoretical perspectives on work design: sociotechnical systems theory, the job characteristics model, process improvement, technostructural change models, activity theory, and adaptive structuration theory. Each theory is examined for its ability to explain work design in new work environments and is shown to offer a different perspective on the design of work. Finally, the implications for further research on work design theory and for the practice of HRD are discussed.

Work design shapes the context of work through traditional structural means and through the reciprocal relationship of structure and human agency (Miller & Droge, 1986). New work environments are characterized by complex, nonlinear dynamics (Weick, 1990) in which the mutual dependence on structure and action means that structure is both a medium and outcome of practice (Giddens, 1979). Action triggers change, intended and unintended, that influences interdependent actors and creates structure. Work activity unfolds within a context that reflects the residuals of prior work activities. In other words, actions are embedded in the structures they generate. In this sense, the term *structure* is used synonymously in this article with *context* as they apply to the work environment. Work design is a primary catalyst of context, and, conversely, the context of work reflects structural dimensions. The role of structure in creating context is similar to adaptive structuration (DeSanctis & Poole, 1994), in which rules and resources from technology and other structures are incorporated into action. Within this broader meaning of structure, *work design* is defined as the systemic organization, design, and articulation of work activities at one or more levels of the organization: systemwide, process, group, job, and task. Work design can occur at any point along the continuum between systemwide work structures and the design of individual tasks. The environment or context within which work design occurs is the work environment.

## Theories Selected for the Review

Six theoretical perspectives on work design were selected for review and critique in this study. Three criteria were used to select theories for the study:

- The theory's main purpose includes explaining the organization and design of work.
- The theory applies to one or more of the following domains of work: systemwide, process, group, job, or task.
- The theory includes both human and technical concepts to explain work design.

Theories were selected that address work design ranging in scope from task design to organization-wide work design and that range in age from ten to more than fifty years old. The theories reviewed are sociotechnical systems theory, the job characteristics model, process improvement, technostructural change models, activity theory, and adaptive structuration theory.

Work design is central to the purpose of these six theories and provides the basis for the interaction of key conceptual elements of them. Sociotechnical systems theory, the job characteristics model, process improvement, and technostructural change models are work design frameworks that have been discussed frequently in HRD and related literatures. Activity theory has only recently been considered as a potentially valuable theory for HRD and related disciplines (Ardichvili, 2003; Engestrom, 2000). Adaptive structuration theory has received little or no attention in the HRD literature despite its power to explain adaptations to technology as key factors in organizational change (DeSanctis & Poole, 1994). Other theories were eliminated from consideration for this study because their primary theoretical domains did not include work design. Among them were human capital theory (Becker, 1993), institutional theory (Zucker, 1987), agency theory (Eisenhardt, 1989), and transaction cost theory (Jones & Hill, 1988). The domains over which these theories apply would have to be artificially stretched to include work design. Conversely, the theories supporting organizational transformation (Miller & Friesen, 1984; Tushman & Romanelli, 1985) and contingency theory (Schoonhoven, 1981) embrace all dimensions of the organization and its environment (philosophy, culture, strategy, environmental contingencies, and structure) and exceed the scope of work design theory. Each of the six theories chosen for this study is reviewed next.

*Sociotechnical Systems Theory.* As first conceptualized by Eric Trist during his work at the Tavistock Institute for Human Relations in London, sociotechnical systems (STS) theory was clearly influenced by an early publication of von Bertalanffy's open systems theories (Trist & Bamforth, 1951). STS theory seeks to enhance job satisfaction and improve productivity through a design process that focuses on the interdependencies between and among people, technology, and the work environment (Emery & Trist, 1969). The recognition that production processes were systems fundamentally composed of human and technological elements led to work designs based on STS theory that were responsive to both the task requirements of the technology and the social and psychological needs of employees (Trist, 1981; Trist, Higgin, Murray & Pollock, 1963). The overarching goal of this approach is the joint optimization of the social and technical aspects of work design.

Early implementations of the STS approach to work design demonstrated its value for enriching jobs and improving productivity in coal mining (Trist & Bamforth, 1951; Mills, 1976), automotive plants (Junsson & Lank, 1985), an Indian weaving mill (Rice, 1953), the shipping industry (Thorsrud, 1968), and other industrial environments (Rice, 1958; Macy, 1980). Also relevant to HRD are subsequent applications of STS that served as the basis for conceptualizing self-managed teams, (Pasmore, Francis, Haldeman, & Shani, 1982), the redesign of work for productivity improvements (Cummings & Molloy, 1977), and as a framework for understanding the dependencies among ideal work design features and the relative impact of choosing not to implement one ideal feature on the effectiveness of other ideal features (Majchrzak, 1997). Recent applications of STS theory underlie innovative work designs and team-based structures that are now prevalent in organizations (Cherns, 1987; Lawler, Mohrman, & Ledford, 1998; Reese, 1995).

Sociotechnical systems thinking has also been applied at the macrolevel to community and environmental issues. According to Heller (1997), Eric Trist first conceptualized STS theory in extraorganizational terms as a model for integrating human and technological elements for environmental and ecological purposes. However, the macrolevel application of STS research was hindered by the exigent priorities imposed by the opportunities and demands of fieldwork in three British coalmines. Nonetheless, extraorganizational applications are evident in early STS theory research (Emery & Trist, 1969) and in Emery and Trist's book, *Toward a Social Ecology* (1973).

Despite the persistence of STS theory, it has been criticized for offering little in the way of prescriptions for how to design work, relying instead on general principles for achieving sociotechnical work environments (Kelly, 1992). In addition, new organizational paradigms suggest that the application of sociotechnical principles alone is insufficient, since design innovations at the subunit level are unlikely to survive if the organization as a whole is not aligned systemically in the same way (Frei, Hugentobler, Schurman, Duell, & Alioth, 1993). According to critics of the theory, more explicit attention to organizational culture and values is needed (Parker & Wall, 1998).

*Job Characteristics Model.* Among the models of work design derived from STS theory, perhaps the most influential is the job characteristics model (Hackman & Oldham, 1980). The job characteristics model (JCM) is among the most well-known and complete theories for explaining job design characteristics and their relationships to work motivation. According to this theory, any job can be described in terms of the following five core job dimensions: skill variety, task identity, task significance, autonomy, and feedback. Seen as being more motivating and satisfying to workers who perform jobs with these characteristics, the five core job dimensions influence psychological states of workers that are more likely to lead to favorable work outcomes: high work productivity and low absenteeism and turnover. The theory further asserts that people with high growth needs are more likely to experience the psychological states with motivating jobs than are people with weaker growth needs. In addition to the JCM itself, Hackman and Oldham (1980) developed the Job Diagnostics Survey, an instrument for measuring the motivation potential of jobs and for guiding work redesign projects.

Since its development more than twenty-five years ago, the JCM has spawned an impressive body of related research on work design. Campion and Thayer (1985) extended Hackman and Oldham's work by developing the Multimethod Job Design Questionnaire (MJDQ), a job design instrument with scales to assess the motivational, biomechanistic, and perceptual-motor aspects of jobs. Other extensions and refinements of the JCM include modifications of the original job diagnostics survey to produce more reliable data (Fried, 1991; Johns, Xie, & Fang, 1992), studies of the relative effects of job redesign on attitudinal versus behavioral outcomes (Kelly, 1992; Parker & Wall, 1998), the addition of achievement motivation and job longevity as moderators to the JCM (Arnold & House, 1980), cross-cultural applications of the JCM (Welsh, Luthans, & Sommer, 1993), revisions to the critical psychological states component of the model (Renn & Vandenburg, 1995), studies of the effects of work context (for example, lack of privacy, high worker densities) on job satisfaction (Parker & Wall, 1998), a framework for job design in which employees actively craft their jobs (Wrzesniewski & Dutton, 2001), and meta-analyses of the effects of the JCM on motivation, satisfaction, and performance (Fried & Ferris, 1987; Loher, Noe, Moeller, & Fitzpatrick, 1985). As these studies demonstrate, the JCM has had a persistent influence on work design thinking and has catalyzed an impressive array of related research.

*Process Improvement.* An organization's work, whether product or service related, is accomplished through a series of phases, or processes, during which value is added. As a value chain for accomplishing work, the work process is a major component of the organization's structure and function and a key element in work design. Davenport (1993) defined a work process as "a structured, measured set of activities designed to produce a specified output for a particular customer or market. . . . A process is a specific ordering of work activities *across time and place* [italics added], with a beginning, an end, and clearly identified inputs and outputs: a structure for action" (p. 5). Davenport's notion that work activities can span across time and space is an important observation because it expands the scope of a work process beyond a single functional area. Indeed, major work processes such as customer order processing and new product development require activities that draw on multiple functional areas. Those that span the boundaries between organizational units are called cross-functional processes.

Process improvement, a major tenet of quality improvement theory, derives from the notion that understanding how work is accomplished during various phases of the process is the key to successful efforts to improve or redesign work. Quality improvement theory is based on the work of Walter Shewhart (1931), W. Edwards Deming (1986), and Joseph Juran (1974). Quality improvement theory espouses a management philosophy that orients all of an organization's activities around the concept of quality. Quality improvement is based on a diverse body of knowledge composed of theory and methods for continuous quality improvement, statistical measurement, process improvement, employee involvement, and education and training. According to quality improvement theory, in order for process improvement to occur, there must be agreement as to what constitutes a work process, that is, the work activities that are specifically included in the process. Work processes that have an identifiable flow or structure, whether they are small, discrete processes or more elaborate, cross-functional processes, can be analyzed and improved using methods such as statistical process control. Process improvement based in quality improvement theory provides employees with the information and decision-making power to make process changes, it is a continuous process (improvement efforts never end), and it increases both employee well-being and organizational productivity (Shetty, 1986). Indeed, continuous process improvement is the primary vehicle for work redesign in organizations that follow the quality improvement philosophy (Garvin, 1988).

*Technostructural Change Models.* Technostructural change models affect change by reconfiguring the organization's technology and structure. Technostructural change models evolved from consideration of the factors thought to be key determinants of organizational structure. Early theories explained that organizational structure was largely a function of contextual factors such as organization size, environment, technology, or scale of operation (Galbraith, 1970). These theories offered the simplest theoretical explanation of how organization design was related to structural variables, which were assumed to be influenced by particular, primarily economic, constraints (Pugh, Hickson, Hinings, & Turner, 1969). Structural models then were developed based on research showing that organizations that faced dynamic markets and technological environments were more economically successful with flexible, organic organizational structures, while organizations in relatively stable environments were more successful with highly structured organizations (Lawrence & Lorsch, 1967). Early studies of the introduction of technology and its effects on organization design showed that computer-based automation promoted the specialization of expertise, facilitated the movement toward process technologies, increased ratios of supervisory and staff personnel, and decentralized authority away from headquarters to individual plant locations (Blau, Falbe, McKinley, & Tracy, 1976; Adler, 1992). Subsequent theories have emphasized the importance of strategic decision making as a necessary precursor to organizational structure and work design (Child, 1972; Miles & Snow, 1978; Mintzberg, 1994).

Technostructural change is receiving increased attention with the current emphasis on organizational effectiveness and sustained competitive advantage. Technostructural change is large-scale change brought about through deliberate attempts to change an organization or subunit toward a different and more effective state by altering its structure and technology (Cummings & Worley, 2001; Galbraith, 1977). Since they focus on structure and technology as major determinants of the environment within which people work, technostructural change models are frequently used to complement other interventions that affect change primarily through social processes and HRD. Technostructural change models are used to design or redesign major processes or work units or to restructure entire organizations; they are of broader scope than the work design models discussed previously. They embrace a set of interventions that include models for functional design, downsizing and work reengineering, and recent structural designs including self-contained units, matrix organizations, and network-based structures (Cummings & Worley, 2001).

Functional design continues to be the most widely used organizational structure in the world today. This is the pyramidal structure with senior management at the top, middle and supervisory management spread out below, and the rest of the nonmanagement workforce at the bottom. As seen in specialized functional units such as marketing and sales, engineering, and accounting and finance, functional design promotes the specialization of skills and resources, allows specialists to share their expertise, and enhances career development within one's functional specialty. Care must be taken with functional designs that departmental outputs are integrated with the contributions of other units to enhance the performance of the organization as a whole. Downsizing is a model for organizational restructuring intended to reduce the size of the organization and cut costs primarily through reductions in the workforce. Reduction in organizational size can occur through any one or a combination of layoffs, attrition, redeployment, reduction in management levels, early retirement, outsourcing, reorganization, divestiture, or delayering (Cascio, 1993; McKinley, Sanchez, & Schick, 1995). In most cases downsizing is associated with greater use of the contingent workforce. Temporary or permanent part-time employees are needed since the reduction in the workforce is not matched by a corresponding reduction in workload; fewer employees must accomplish the same amount of work.

Work reengineering is a radical approach to organizational restructuring that replaces the existing work structure with a completely new design, and since jobs are eliminated through work reengineering, it also results in fewer employees (Hammer & Champy, 1993). Work is reengineered by literally starting over and redesigning it from scratch. It requires the redesign of work processes and the integration of tasks to eliminate the errors, delays, and rework that are associated with having different people do different parts of the same process. In order for work reengineering to result in fewer jobs, called the horizontal reorganization of work, vertical reorganization of work is also needed. Those who remain after jobs are eliminated are expected to handle broader tasks and make more decisions.

Recent structural designs include self-contained units, matrix organizations, and network-based structures. Self-contained units group organizational activities on the basis of products, services, customers, or geography. They are typically set up with all or most of the resources needed to accomplish their specific objectives and are often created, either temporarily or permanently, to handle a specific product, service, customer, or region. The matrix organization is an attempt to maximize the strengths and minimize the weaknesses of both the functional and self-contained unit structures. It superimposes the lateral structure of a product or project coordinator on a vertical functional structure. The matrix organization evolved to deal with environments in which changing customer demands and technological conditions caused managers to focus on lateral relationships between functions to develop a flexible and adaptable system of resources and procedures and to achieve multiple project objectives (Kolodny, 1981). Network-based structures redraw organizational boundaries and link separate organizations to facilitate task interaction. In network-based structures, functions that are traditionally performed within a single organization are performed by different network members. The essence of networks is the arrangement of relationships between organizations so that each organization handles what it does best (Powell, 1990). Often used as the basis for joint ventures and other collaborative relationships between organizations, networks are considered to be uniquely suited to deal with complex, dynamic interorganizational exchanges since they allow for vertical disaggregration and flexible coordination across participating organizations (Achrol, 1997).

***Activity Theory.*** Activity theory explains purposeful behavior by focusing on the structure of the activity itself (Leont'ev, 1978, 1981). Rather than viewing the mind or behavior as the primary object of analysis, activity theory focuses on the actual processes of interaction in which humans engage with the world and each other. It is rooted in the work of preeminent Soviet psychologist Lev Vygotsky and the concept of *deyatel'nost,* a term with meaning similar to that associated with the Western notion of activity. In a significant departure from Western views at the time, Vygotsky believed that mental functioning could be understood only by going outside the individual to examine the sociocultural processes from which it derives—a conception of cognition that removed the distinction between internal mental processes and the external world (Vygotsky, 1978). Leont'ev, one of Vygotsky's first students, developed a coherent and integrated framework for activity theory. Activity theory has recently been applied to work and can serve as a flexible framework for the conceptualization of work activity.

At the core of activity theory is the concept of activity as a unit of analysis that includes both the individual and his or her culturally defined environment. From Leont'ev's perspective, "the psychological experiment can no longer be set up entirely to model philosophical speculation: it must model the phenomena of everyday, practical activity" (Cole, 1981, p. ix). Leont'ev conceived of activity as systems of organized units for performing mental functions involving the individual and others engaged in the same activity within a culturally defined environment (Leont'ev, 1978, 1981). The environment is not seen simply as a means of getting access to the individual, but as an integral element of the activity itself. This multidimensional conception of activity, which takes the environment into account, is the basis of activity theory and is considered to be the appropriate unit of analysis for human behavior.

According to the theory, an activity can be analyzed at three levels. First, at the highest level of organization is the motivation of the activity itself, a broader concept than in Western thinking, closer in meaning to that of strategy than task. Activities are distinguished on the basis of their motive and the object toward which they are oriented. At the next level are goal-directed actions, a flexible system of actions for accomplishing the activity that can incorporate various methods and patterns. At the third level are operations, or the specific conditions under which goal-directed actions are carried out. For example, if our action is traveling from one place to another in the service of some activity (for example, pursuing leisure and recreation), whether we walk, drive, or use some other means of transportation is an operation that depends on distance and other conditions related to the action.

The dynamic relationships among these three elements of activity theory provide a flexible framework for better understanding the design of work environments. Activities, actions, and operations may change positions in the hierarchy relative to one another according to changing situations, new knowledge, and the intention of human agents. Since activities, actions, and operations are defined according to their functions rather than properties inherent in the elements themselves, an activity can lose its motivating force and become an action in the service of another activity (for example, losing interest in the intrinsic value of one's job and performing it primarily for income). Hence, the theory allows work activity to be studied at different levels of analysis: the activity, the action, and the operation. Since activity is conceptualized as a dynamic system, methods of studying activity can change as the activity changes and as new questions about it emerge. Conceptualizing work activity using activity theory allows designers to use the work design process to bridge from the present to the desired work environment and to move easily across levels of activity as dictated by the design process. The malleability of activity theory provides a flexible framework for the study of work activity.

Although limited in number, applications of activity theory to the study of work design and HRD include Scribner's study (1984) of the practical thinking strategies used by workers to economize on mental and physical effort, Engestrom's examination (2000) of work redesign in a Finnish pediatric health care facility, and Ardichvili's proposal (2003) that activity theory be used as a basis for developing socially situated learning experiences considered to be especially useful for work-related education and training.

*Adaptive Structuration Theory.* Adaptive structuration theory is a framework for studying the variations in organizational change that occur as advanced technologies are implemented and used (DeSanctis & Poole, 1994). According to adaptive structuration theory, adaptation of technology by organizational actors is a key factor in organizational change that can be examined from two vantage points: the types of structures that are provided by advanced technologies and the structures that actually emerge in human action as people interact with these technologies. The term *structures* refers to the general rules and resources that guide human activity in organizations such as reporting hierarchies, organizational knowledge, and standard operating procedures. The act of bringing the rules and resources from an advanced technology or other structural sources into action is termed *structuration.* Since actual behavior when using advanced technologies frequently differs from intended use, adaptive structuration theory is embraced by researchers who believe that the effects of advanced technologies are as much a function of the properties inherent in the technologies as of how they are used by people. The theory focuses on the interplay between two types of structures, intended and actual, to gain a deeper understanding of the processes through which advanced technologies are implemented and the impacts of advanced technologies on organizations.

The structuration process can be captured by isolating a group's application of a specific technology-based rule or resource within a specific context and at a specific point in time. The immediate, visible actions that indicate deeper structuration processes are called *appropriations* of the technology. By examining appropriations, we can uncover exactly how a given rule or resource within a specific technology is brought into action. Technology structures become stabilized in the interactions of a work group if the group appropriates them in a consistent way, reproducing them in similar form over time. Once emergent structures are used and accepted, they may become institutions in their own right and the change is fixed in the organization (DeSanctis & Poole, 1994).

Adaptive structuration theory posits that four major sources of structure—technology, task, environment, and the work group's internal system—affect social interaction. Work design features are present in these sources of structure. Work design is represented in technology structures that enable innovations or improvements to existing work methods (for example, technical innovations in electronic messaging or group decision support). It is reflected in a given work task, since existing work practices must be altered to allow for the use of new or modified resources. Resources and constraints afforded by the organizational environment (such as budgets, political pressures, history of task accomplishment, and cultural beliefs) also reflect the overall design of work. Since adaptive structuration theory identifies structures that emerge in human action as people adapt to technology, it can offer new insights into the relationship between work design as intended by designers and how a new design structure influences the work practices that emerge over time. Workers naturally discern the valuable features of new designs while bypassing other features made available by designers. Work practices evolve as users modify their activities to technical innovations.

Empirical studies using adaptive structuration theory include Orlikowski, Yates, Okamura, and Fujimoto's study (1995) of the implementation of a computer conferencing system in a Japanese research and development project; Chin, Gopal, and Salisbury's development and validation (1997) of a measurement scale to assess the appropriations of advanced technology structures by users; and Griffith's use (1999) of adaptive structuration theory as the basis of a model of sense making of new technologies. Adaptive structuration theory and subsequent empirical studies based on the theory have advanced our knowledge of organization development and change and the role of technology implementation in change processes.

## Discussion

Each of these six theories—STS theory, the job characteristics model, process improvement, technostructural change models, activity theory, and adaptive structuration theory—serves a particular purpose for explaining the organization and design of work. Each emerged during a different time period to address needs related to particular concerns about the organization and design of work at that time:

Responding to mid-twentieth-century concerns about the effects of advancements in manufacturing technologies on people and productivity, STS theory offered a fundamentally new perspective on the organization of work—work design for joint optimization of its social and technical dimensions.

The job characteristics model established specific task design characteristics and the conditions under which they enhance work motivation and work-related outcomes.

Grounded in quality improvement theory, process improvement derives from the notion that understanding how work is accomplished and flows through the organization is the key to successful efforts to improving or redesigning work processes.

Several technostructural change models have emerged to address the need for different types of work structures, including traditional structural and functional designs. Recent designs such as matrix organizations and network based structures address complex organizational and environmental dynamics.

Adaptive structural theory attempts to explain variations in organizational change that occur as new technologies are introduced and adapted for use.

Recently applied to work activity, activity theory and its conceptual levels—activities, actions, and operations—allow a flexible framework for the conceptualization of work activity.

In short, each theory arose within a particular sociohistorical context to meet a specific purpose related to concerns about the organization and performance of work at that time. These theories continue to guide our thinking about work design. Some do so by aiding our understanding of work design issues present in today's work environments (adaptive structuration theory, process improvement, technostructural change models), some earlier theories have shaped current thinking on work design (STS theory, the JCM), and some hold promise as future explanations of the design of work (activity theory).

Each theory varies in the scope of its application to work design in organizations. Work design theories can be construed broadly into categories according to their scope of application (Frei et al., 1993). Three levels of application that apply to all organizations are systemwide, intermediate, and individual (Rashford & Coghlan, 1994). The intermediate range of the scale lies between systemwide and job- or task-specific and encompasses teams, functional groups, departments, divisions, and other subunits of the system. A continuum using these levels to show the scope of application of work design theories appears in Figure 1.

Each work design theory was formulated to cover a domain of knowledge broad enough to support the theory's distinctive contributions to knowledge of work design. Consistent with its purpose, each theory varies in the scope of its application to work design from systemwide (technostructural change) to job- or task-design specific (job characteristics model). Technostructural change theory applies to entire systems (such as organizations) and major subsystems. The job characteristics model applies to the design of jobs and tasks. Thus,

### Figure 1. Scope of Application of Work Design Theories

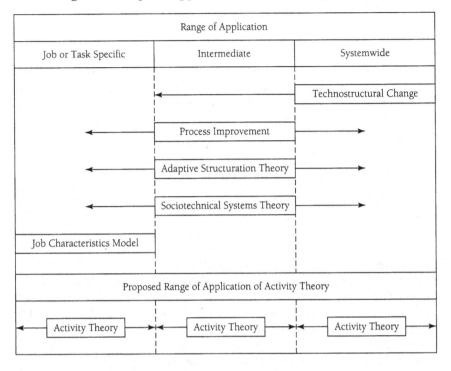

technostructural change and the job characteristics model have different scopes of application to work design and are shown at opposite ends of the continuum in Figure 1.

Adaptive structuration theory is potentially relevant to any work setting affected by technology-triggered change. Similarly, STS theory supports work design intended to jointly optimize social and technical design issues in a broad range of workplaces. Each of these theories can be applied at the job or task, intermediate, or systemwide levels. Although they potentially apply across the organization, STS theory and adaptive structuration theory most often explain the design of organizational subsystems (intermediate range). Process improvement also applies to the intermediate range of the scale between systemwide and job or task specific since it is an approach to improving or redesigning work processes, a construct at the intermediate range. Since these three theories can explain both intermediate-range work designs and job or systemwide work designs concurrently (for example, explaining how a job fits with a cross-functional process to which the job contributes), arrows appear in Figure 1 pointing to the left and right indicating these scopes of application for the three intermediate-range theories.

The scope of application of activity theory to work design has not been addressed explicitly in the literature. It is proposed that this theory applies to the full range of the continuum shown in Figure 1. Since the domain of activity theory embraces activities, actions, and operations and can include one or more levels of work activity, the theory can potentially apply to work issues at the job or task, intermediate, or systemwide levels. Since activity can be used at any level or combination of adjacent levels in Figure 1, it can facilitate the integration of work design across levels. Conceptualizing work activity using activity theory allows designers to move easily across levels of activity as dictated by the design process.

## Critique and Implications for Further Research

Two concerns emerge from this discussion about the explanations of work design offered by these theories. First, these theories do not provide an adequate conceptual foundation for work design in new work environments, including virtual and alternative work environments, that are increasingly common (Bailey & Kurland, 2002; Liker, Haddad, & Karlin, 1999). They explain work designs of the past better than they explain how to design work for some present and future settings. Second, since these theories were developed for particular purposes and applications (such as job design or restructuring), they explain work design in ways that allow discontinuities in how work is structured and articulated between and among organizational levels. These concerns and their implications for further research on work design theory are discussed next.

*The Changing Nature of Work.* The notion of work discussed in this article does not assume a separation of work from other aspects of life. Work-life integration brings one's work activities and life activities (nonwork) into a mutually reinforcing balance (Friedman, Christensen, & DeGroot, 1998). The distinction between work and nonwork has been blurred since the structure and location of work has been altered by the increasing prevalence of flexible work situations that are not time and place specific (Bridges, 1994; Smith, 1997). These new work situations include virtual work (Hill, Miller, & Weiner, 1998) and the emergence of the alternative workplace (Apgar, 1998). Flexible structures are appealing to organizations that are responding to hypercompetitive business environments (Volberda, 1998). Reflecting the movement toward more flexible employment relationships sought by both employees and employers, the alternative workplace represents a multitude of locations where work can be accomplished other than the traditional office or shop floor (Apgar, 1998). Virtual work is associated with the terms *telework* and *telecommuting,* although each of these has a different meaning. *Telework* is a broad term for doing one's job away from the office through the use of telecommunications equipment (Hill et al., 1998). *Telecommuting* (Potter, 2003) was introduced to emphasize that telework could eventually replace the daily commute. Unlike most telecommuters who have a fixed alternative worksite at home, virtual work and the virtual office refer to situations in which workers have the flexibility to work from a variety of locations.

Recent research has compared virtual with traditional work environments on a variety of perceptual and business measures. Studies have found that resistance to telecommuting can originate from managers who rely on traditional line-of-sight management styles (Potter, 2003), that telecommuting can reduce costs but also may result in the need to alter management practices (Watad & DiSanzo, 2000), and that virtual reality systems can improve certain dimensions of the telecommuting experience (Venkatesh & Johnson, 2002). Hill et al. (1998) found that use of the virtual office was significantly related to higher productivity and greater flexibility, but not to work-life balance, morale, and other perceptions of employee well-being.

Studies of the consequences of organizational restructuring show that managers and subordinates should not be expected to have the same reactions to a new organizational structure (Luthans & Sommer, 1999) and that the sense of purpose felt by managers as a result of restructuring may not be shared by subordinates (McKinley & Scherer, 2000). Thus, although alternative work designs can reduce operating costs, this may occur at the expense of creativity (Amabile & Conti, 1999), innovation (Dougherty & Bowman, 1995), employee morale (Hill et al., 1998), organizational connectedness (Raghuram, Garud, Wiesenfeld, & Gupta (2001), and other indicators of employee well-being (Fisher & White, 2000).

Recent work design developments go beyond the notion of the alternative workplace. For an increasing number of workers, the work environment is characterized not only by alternative work settings but also by frequent change in setting and geographical location. Enabled by ever more sophisticated technology, many workers now migrate between several work settings depending on what setting is most advantageous for conducting the task at hand. One can work from home, from multiple office locations, and on the road virtually unbounded by geographical location. This represents a new polymorphic work environment in which continuous change is possible; the work setting can change frequently and continuously depending on business-related needs. This fluidity of work settings represents a fundamental departure from traditional work environments and from fixed alternative worksites, such as at home.

Organizations continue to respond to the appeal of these new, alternative work designs to get work done more efficiently. The time and cost savings from instituting alternative work designs are readily apparent to managers and have a significant influence on work design decisions. However, beyond their short-term effects, much remains unknown about these work environments, a situation exacerbated by the continually changing nature of these environments. Postimplementation studies to assess the merits of instituting new work designs often show that the trade-offs and consequences of alternative work environments, both beneficial and detrimental, become apparent only after investing in these changes (Cascio, Young, & Morris, 1997; Fisher & White, 2000; Hill et al., 1998; McKinley & Scherer, 2000; Parker, Wall, & Jackson, 1997). This occurs in part because relevant theories and models for decision making are not yet available to inform work design considerations when they are initially conceived.

Indeed, the social reality of work design and technology implementation is quite complex (Liker et al., 1999). The efficacy of work redesign is influenced by many factors, including economics, management philosophy, labor-management relations, the degree of shared agreement about how the work is reorganized, and the process through which new work designs and technology are implemented (Salvendy & Karwowski, 1994). On what basis do we separate employees physically and temporally from the organization when considering the use of virtual and alternative work environments? How are those who work in environments that are not time and place specific expected to relate to their work, each other, and the organization? How should the design of work for these environments be conceived and implemented? How well does existing work design theory address these questions?

Although existing theory provides some insight into this area, it seems insufficient for providing a full understanding of these new work environments. The theories reviewed here do not adequately explain how to organize, design, and articulate work activities for flexible work situations that are not time and place specific:

STS theory emphasizes the design of work to optimize the match between the task requirements of the technology and the social and psychological needs of employees. But how are such work designs conceived in virtual environments where workers may experience physical and psychological separation from others?

Although the JCM shows how worker productivity and motivation can be enhanced by emphasizing five core job dimensions, this theory was never intended to explain how to design these job dimensions (skill variety, task identity, task significance, autonomy, and feedback) in work environments characterized by the geographical and temporal separation of the worker from supervisors and others.

The principles of process improvement were developed for service and manufacturing processes deeply rooted in the technology and infrastructure of specific commercial applications. Workers are now less reliant on the support and resources afforded by a fixed work environment.

Activity theory has been applied only recently to work settings, and although it may prove useful for explaining how to design work activities in the future, no known studies have applied activity theory to virtual or alternative work environments.

Traditional work design models were not developed for what, at the time of their development, would have been considered futuristic work environments. How should designers respond to the unpredictability and changing nature of these work settings? Would better work designs emerge from theory influenced by constructivist thinking (Gergen, 1999)? Could social constructionist theory offer a richer explanation of how work experience is created and given meaning by those who perform it (Turnbull, 2002)? What explanations can be offered for the effects these new work environments have on the worker, relevant others, and the performance of the work itself? Better theory is needed to support work design for these new environments.

***The Need for Multilevel Work Design Theory.*** As defined in this article, work design can occur at any point along the continuum from systemwide work structures to the design of work at the job and task levels. Organizing and aligning work activities across organizational levels is a challenging endeavor due to the many considerations involved in the integration of these work activities. Translating strategic initiatives into operational terms involves accommodating contingencies and optimizing multiple, often competing requirements at several operational levels (Mintzberg, 1994). The mission and goals of the organization must be conceptually and operationally related to work design, even though the linkage of strategic goals to supporting work structures may not be immediate or complete (Holton, 1999; Miles & Snow, 1978). Nonetheless, when discontinuity occurs in work design across levels, it is readily apparent to employees. Staw and Boettger (1990) studied the problem of task revision and illustrated the relationship of work design to employee performance. They manipulated actual tasks to contain erroneous information and showed that participants had little natural tendency toward task revision and a high level of conformity to established procedures, especially those reinforced by organizational hierarchy and control systems, even when tasks contained obviously erroneous content. They demonstrated that inconsistencies across levels in work structures and requirements can impede employee performance.

Unfortunately, existing theory explains work design in ways that allow inconsistency and discontinuity across system levels. This occurs when multidimensional phenomena are conceptualized in ways that ignore their systemic implications. Existing work design models were not developed for the systemwide organization and design of work. As shown in Figure 1, each of the six theories has a different scope of application. Technostructural change models address the systemwide organization of work, the job characteristics model addresses work design at the job and task levels, and the remaining theories in Figure 1 address intermediate levels of the system. Designs that are work unit-specific ignore systemwide interdependencies (Galbraith & Lawler, 1993), and fail to address the systemic alignment of reward systems with performance (Rummler & Brache, 1995). Other models of work design apply to jobs (Ilgen & Hollenbeck, 1992) and groups (Hackman, 1990; Guzzo & Dickson, 1996). None of the theories provides the conceptual basis for work design frameworks that are integrated across system-level strategy, operations, and, ultimately, job and task requirements.

These concerns about the design and articulation of work across levels can be addressed by developing multilevel work design theory. Such theory provides a framework for the design of work that relates to multiple levels of the organization. Developing multilevel theory requires the consideration of both the structure and function of constructs as they apply to work design.

***Joint Consideration of Construct Structure and Function.*** The development of multilevel work design theory requires consideration of both the structure and function of work design constructs since each dimension of the construct provides a different perspective on the construct's utility for multilevel theory (Morgeson & Hofmann, 1999). A focus on the structure of work design constructs tends to highlight the differences across levels. For example, job design, which reflects the task specification and resource needs of the individual, is structurally dissimilar from cross-functional process design, which must account for multiple, functional transactions and contingencies. The structure of the construct alone does not allow for the cross-level comparison of work design features since it emphasizes the differences between levels. Explicit consideration of the construct's function allows integration of functionally similar (but structurally dissimilar) constructs into broader networks of constructs. Since organizational structures can be purposefully designed to yield outputs (information, programs, products, services, and so on) that are compatible across levels regardless of the level at which the work occurs, work designs can be structurally dissimilar yet yield outputs that are consistent from level to level. Theoretical emphasis is placed on the joint consideration of construct structure and function when developing multilevel theory. Multilevel work design theory requires the analysis of both the structure and function of work design constructs.

Measurement is another important consideration in the development of multilevel work design theory since theorists must consider both conceptual and measurement issues when operationalizing constructs (Klein, Dansereau, & Hall, 1994). Since a multilevel theory of work design is expected to explain the organization of work across levels of the system, measures of work design are needed that can be applied to two or more system levels simultaneously. However, most measures of work outcomes and processes apply to specific levels of the system only (measures of job output, departmental performance, plant productivity, and so on). Existing instruments and measures of work design include Hackman and Oldham's job diagnostic survey (1980); Campion and Thayer's MJDQ (1985); the measures of job control, cognitive demand, and production responsibility developed by Jackson, Wall, Martin, and Davids (1993); measures of work design dependencies (Majchrzak, 1997); statistical measures to assess variance in process quality (Gitlow & Hertz, 1983); measures of work redesign for information technology in advanced manufacturing (Parker & Wall, 1998); and assessments of the psychometric properties of the MJDQ (Edwards, Scully, & Brtek, 1999). Each of these measures has been developed to assess work-related phenomena at a specific level of the system only (Jackson et al., 1993). Measures of work design constructs that apply to two or more system levels simultaneously are needed to test and refine a multilevel work design framework. They may be based on the resources and materials needed for work, process requirements, cross-functional transactions, temporal considerations for work, information characteristics, structural requirements, work outputs, and other dimensions of the work. They will help to measure work design interrelationships across levels for a better understanding of this phenomenon.

Theorists need not start from scratch when developing multilevel work design theory. Activity theory provides a framework for work design that can potentially apply to any systems level or combination of levels. This theory embraces activities, actions, and operations and can be applied to work issues at the job or task, intermediate, or systemwide level. Conceptualizing work activity using activity theory allows designers to move easily across levels of activity as dictated by the design process. Thus, activity theory is proposed as a basis for the further development of multilevel work design theory.

***Implications for Human Resource Development Practice.*** Those who are responsible for employee development cannot afford to lose sight of recent developments in work design since many new skills in need of development emerge from changes in work design. Ample evidence exists in the literature cited here of the discontinuity in theories that address multilevel phenomena. HRD scholars have also acknowledged the need for theory that reflects the multilevel integration of systemic phenomena in areas such as performance domains (Holton, 1999), organizational structure and strategy (Semler, 1997), individual and organizational learning (Confessore & Kops, 1998), learning and performance improvement (Torraco, 2000), and the vertical integration of HRD in organizations (Wognum, 2000). These studies demonstrate the importance of theory that enables the multilevel integration of systemic phenomena in HRD.

Multilevel work design theory can generate models for decision making that improve HRD practice. Coordination among work units for shared resources means that work design changes at one level affect the design of work in other areas. Organizational goals shape work processes requirements, which in turn influence the knowledge and capabilities needed by employees who contribute to these processes. Opportunities for HRD exist at all levels— individual, group, process, and systemwide. Since work design changes have multiple effects and important needs for HRD emerge from these changes, HRD practice can be more effective when framed as a systemic intervention informed by multilevel theory. Multilevel work design theory is needed that reflects the conceptual, analytical, and measurement issues discussed here.

Better theories of work design are also needed because of the negative implications for employee development of poorly articulated work designs. Engagement in learning by the most committed employees can be wasted when the application of what is learned to the workplace is hindered by poorly designed work environments (Tracey, Tannenbaum, & Kavanaugh, 1995). HRD scholars are cognizant of the social, psychological, and organizational influences on employee learning and performance and are well positioned to use this expertise to develop theory that supports effective work design. Since they study the development of managers and employees at all levels of the organization, HRD scholars recognize the need for work systems that enable seamless performance across levels of the organization so that employee development has beneficial results.

Implications for HRD also arise from changes in work reflected in virtual and alternative work environments. The preparation of those who work in these environments should now include consideration of the opportunities and challenges of employment both in and outside organizations (Hall, 2002). Work environments that are not time and place specific require different skills from those needed in traditional work settings (Apgar, 1998; Kanter, 2001). Although communities of practice can develop in virtual environments, they face unique barriers and prerequisites for success (Ardichvili, Page, & Wentling, 2002). Physical and temporal separation from the major locus of work activity also requires the capability for visualizing situations that are developing elsewhere without sentient cues and information on the events themselves (Torraco, 2002). Today's information-rich work environments require work designs that draw attention to the most important information and place more emphasis on the development of higher-level evaluation and problem-solving skills (Norman, 1993). Finally, the HRD implications of new work environments again underscore the importance of developing a work-force with the capabilities for continuous learning. Learning and sense making are more important than ever before for adapting resourcefully to new environments and unforeseen circumstances.

## References

Achrol, R. (1997). Changes in the theory of interorganizational relations in marketing: Toward a network paradigm. *Journal of the Academy of Marketing Science, 25,* 56–71.

Adler, P. S. (1992). Introduction. In P. S. Adler (Ed.), *Technology and the future of work.* New York: Oxford University Press.

Amabile, T. M., & Conti, R. (1999). Changes in the work environment for creativity during downsizing. *Academy of Management Journal, 42,* 630–640.

Apgar, M. (1998). The alternative workplace: Changing where and how people work. *Harvard Business Review, 62,* 121–136.

Ardichvili, A. (2003). Constructing socially situated learning experiences in human resource development: An activity theory perspective. *Human Resource Development International, 5* (3), 301–325.

Ardichvili, A., Page, V., & Wentling, T. (2002). Virtual knowledge-sharing communities of practice at Caterpillar: Success factor and barriers. *Performance Improvement Quarterly, 15* (3), 94–113.

Arnold, H. J., & House, R. J. (1980). Methodological and substantive extensions of the job characteristics model of motivation. *Organizational Behavior and Human Performance, 25*, 161–183.

Bailey, D. E., & Kurland, N. B. (2002). A review of telework research: Findings, new directions, and lessons for the study of modern work. *Journal of Organizational Behavior, 23*, 383–400.

Barley, S. R., & Orr, J. E. (1997). *Between craft and science: Technical work in U.S. settings.* Ithaca, NY: ILR Press.

Becker, G. S. (1993). *Human capital: A theoretical and empirical analysis with special reference to education* (3rd ed.). Chicago: University of Chicago Press.

Blau, P. M., Falbe, C. M., McKinley, W., & Tracy, P. K. (1976). Technology and organization in manufacturing. *Administrative Science Quarterly, 21*, 20–40.

Bridges, W. (1994, September 19). The end of the job. *Fortune*, 62–74.

Campbell, J. P., McCloy, R. A., Oppler, S. H., & Sager C. E. (1993). A theory of performance. In N. Schmitt & W. C. Borman (Eds.), *Personnel selection in organizations* (pp. 35–70). San Francisco: Jossey-Bass.

Campion, M. A., & Thayer, P. W. (1985). Development and field evaluation of an interdisciplinary measure of job design. *Journal of Applied Psychology, 70*, 29–43.

Cappelli, P., Bassi, L., Katz, H., Knoke, D., Osterman, P., & Useem, M. (1997). *Change at work.* New York: Oxford University Press.

Cascio, W. F. (1993). Downsizing: What do we know? What have we learned? *Academy of Management Executive, 7*, 95–104.

Cascio, W. F., Young, C. E., & Morris, J. R. (1997). Financial consequences of employment change decisions in major U.S. corporations. *Academy of Management Journal, 40*, 1175–1189.

Cherns, A. (1987). Principles of sociotechnical design revisited. *Human Relations, 40*, 153–162.

Child, J. (1972). Organizational structure, environment and performance: The role of strategic choice. *Sociology, 6*, 1–22.

Chin, W. W., Gopal, A., & Salisbury, W. D. (1997). Advancing the theory of adaptive structuration: The development of a scale to measure faithfulness of appropriation. *Information Systems Research, 8*, 342–367.

Cole, M. (1981). Preface. In J. V. Wertsch (Ed.), *The concept of activity in Soviet psychology.* Armonk, NY: M. E. Sharpe.

Confessore, S., & Kops, W. (1998). Self-directed learning and the learning organization. Examining the connection between the individual and the learning environment. *Human Resource Development Quarterly, 9* (4), 365–375.

Cummings, T. G., & Molloy, E. (1977). *Improving productivity and the quality of work life.* New York: Praeger.

Cummings, T. G., & Worley, C. G. (2001). *Organization development and change* (8th ed.). Cincinnati, OH: South-Western College Publishing.

Davenport, T. H. (1993). *Process innovation: Reengineering work through information technology.* Boston: Harvard Business School Press.

Deming, W. E. (1986). *Out of the crisis.* Cambridge, MA: Center for Advanced Engineering Study.

DeSanctis, G., & Poole, M. S. (1994). Capturing the complexity in advanced technology use: Adaptive structuration theory. *Organization Science, 5* (2), 121–147.

Dougherty, D., & Bowman, E. H. (1995). The effects of organizational downsizing on product innovation. *California Management Review, 37* (4), 28–44.

Edwards, J. R., Scully, J. A., & Brtek, M. D. (1999). The measurement of work: Hierarchical representation of the multimethod job design questionnaire. *Personnel Psychology, 52* (2), 305–334.

Eisenhardt, K. M. (1989). Agency theory: An assessment and review. *Academy of Management Review, 14* (2), 488–511.

Emery, F. E., & Trist, E. L. (1969). Sociotechnical systems. In F. E. Emery (Ed.), *Systems thinking* (pp. 281–296). London: Penguin Books.

Emery, F. E., & Trist, E. L. (1973). *Toward a social ecology.* London: Plenum Press.

Engestrom, Y. (2000). Activity theory as a framework for analyzing and redesigning work. *Ergonomics, 43* (7), 960–975.

Fisher, S. R., & White, M. A. (2000). Downsizing in a learning organization: Are there hidden costs? *Academy of Management Review, 25* (1), 244–251.

Frei, F., Hugentobler, M., Schurman, S., Duell, W., & Alioth, A. (1993). *Work design for the competent organization.* Westport, CT: Quorum.

Fried, Y. (1991). Meta-analytic comparison of the job diagnostic survey and job characteristics inventory as correlates of work satisfaction and performance. *Journal of Applied Psychology, 76* (5), 690–697.

Fried, Y., & Ferris G. (1987). The validity of the job characteristics model: A review and meta-analysis. *Personnel Psychology, 40,* 287–322.

Friedman, S. D., Christensen, P., & DeGroot, J. (1998). Work and life: The end of the zero-sum game. *Harvard Business Review, 76* (6), 119–129.

Galbraith, J. R. (1970). Environmental and technological determinants of organizational design. In J. W. Lorsch & P. R. Lawrence (Eds.), *Studies in organizational design.* Homewood, IL: Irwin.

Galbraith, J. R. (1977). *Organization design.* Reading, MA: Addison-Wesley.

Galbraith, J. R., & Lawler, E. F. (1993). *Organizing for the future: The new logic for managing complex organizations.* San Francisco: Jossey-Bass.

Garvin, D. (1988). *Managing quality: The strategic and competitive edge.* New York: Free Press.

Gergen, K. J. (1999). *An invitation to social construction.* Thousand Oaks, CA: Sage.

Giddens, A. (1979). *Central problems in social theory.* Los Angeles: University of California Press.

Gitlow, H. S., & Hertz, P. T. (1983, September–October). Product defects and productivity. *Harvard Business Review,* 131–141.

Griffith, T. L. (1999). Technology features as triggers for sensemaking. *Academy of Management Review, 24* (3), 472–488.

Guzzo, R. A., & Dickson, M. W. (1996). Teams in organizations: Recent research on performance and effectiveness. *Annual Review of Psychology, 47,* 307–338.

Hackman, J. R. (Ed.). (1990). *Teams that work (and those that don't).* San Francisco: Jossey-Bass.

Hackman, J. R., & Oldham, G. R. (1980). *Work redesign.* Reading, MA: Addison-Wesley.

Hall, D. T. (2002). *Careers in and out of organizations.* Thousands Oaks, CA: Sage.

Hammer, M., & Champy, J. (1993). *Reengineering the corporation: A manifesto for business revolution.* New York: HarperCollins.

Heller, F. (1997). Sociotechnology and the environment. *Human Relations, 50* (5), 605–624.

Hill, E. J., Miller, B. C., & Weiner, S. P. (1998). Influences of the virtual office on aspects of work and work/life balance. *Personnel Psychology, 51* (3), 667–683.

Holton, E. F. III (1999). Performance domains and their boundaries. *Advances in Developing Human Resource, 1,* 26–46.

Howard, A. (Ed.). (1995). *The changing nature of work.* San Francisco: Jossey-Bass.

Ilgen, D. R., & Hollenbeck J. R. (1992). The structure of work: Job design and roles. In M. D. Dunnette & L. M. Hough (Eds.), *Handbook of industrial and organizational psychology* (2nd ed., pp. 165–207). Palo Alto, CA: CPP.

Jackson, P. R., Wall, T. D., Martin, R., & Davids, K. (1993). New measures of job control, cognitive demand, and production responsibility. *Journal of Applied Psychology, 78,* 753–762.

Johns, G., Xie, J. L., & Fang, Y. (1992). Mediating and moderating effects on job design. *Journal of Management, 18,* 657–676.

Jones, G., & Hill, C. (1988). Transaction cost analysis of strategy-structure choice. *Strategic Management Journal, 9,* 159–172.

Junsson, B., & Lank, A. G. (1985, Winter). Volvo: A report on the workshop on production technology and quality of working life. *Human Resources Management,* 459–468.

Juran, J. M. (1974). *Quality control handbook* (3rd ed.). New York: McGraw-Hill.

Kanter, R. M. (2001). *E-volve! Succeeding in the digital culture of tomorrow.* Boston: Harvard Business School Press.

Kelly, J. E. (1992). Does job re-design theory explain job re-design outcomes? *Human Relations, 45,* 753–774.

Klein, K. J., Dansereau, F., & Hall, R. J. (1994). Levels issues in theory development, data collection, and analysis. *Academy of Management Review, 19,* 105–229.

Kolodny, H. (1981). Managing in a matrix. *Business Horizons, 24,* 17–35.

Lawler, E., Mohrman, S., & Ledford, G. (1998). *Strategies of high-performance organizations.* San Francisco: Jossey-Bass.

Lawrence, P. R., & Lorsch, J. W. (1967). *Organization and environment: Managing differentiation and integration.* Cambridge, MA: Harvard Graduate School of Business.

Leont'ev, A. N. (1978). *Activity, consciousness, and personality.* Upper Saddle River, NJ: Prentice Hall.

Leont'ev, A. N. (1981). *Problems of the development of mind.* Moscow: Progress Publishers.

Liker, J. K., Haddad, C. J., & Karlin, J. (1999). Perspectives on technology and work organization. *Annual Review of Sociology, 25,* 575–596.

Loher, B. T., Noe, R. A., Moeller, N. L., & Fitzpatrick, M. P. (1985). A meta-analysis of the relation of job characteristics to job satisfaction. *Journal of Applied Psychology, 70* (2), 280–289.

Luff, P., Hindmarsh, J., & Heath, C. (2000). *Workplace studies: Recovering work practice and informing system design.* Cambridge: Cambridge University Press.

Luthans, F., & Sommer, S. M. (1999). The impact of downsizing on work attitudes: Differing reactions of managers and staff in a health care organization. *Group and Organization Management, 24,* 46–70.

Macy, B. A. (1980, July). The quality of work life project at Bolivar. *Monthly Labor Review,* 42–51.

Majchrzak, A. (1997). What to do when you can't have it all: Toward a theory of sociotechnical dependencies. *Human Relations, 50* (5), 535–565.

McKinley, W., Sanchez, C. M., & Schick, A. G. (1995). Organizational downsizing: Constraining, cloning, learning. *Academy of Management Executive, 9* (3), 32–44.

McKinley, W., & Scherer, A. G. (2000). Some unanticipated consequences of organizational restructuring. *Academy of Management Review, 25* (4), 735–752.

Miles, R., & Snow, C. (1978). *Organization strategy, structure, and process.* New York: McGraw-Hill.

Miller, D., & Droge, C. (1986). Psychological and traditional determinants of structure. *Administrative Science Quarterly, 31,* 539–560.

Miller, D., & Friesen, P. (1984). *Organizations: A quantum view.* Upper Saddle River, NJ: Prentice Hall.

Mills, T. (1976, October). Altering the social structure in coal mining: A case study. *Monthly Labor Review,* 3–10.

Mintzberg, H. (1994). *The rise and fall of strategic planning.* New York: Free Press.

Morgeson, F. P., & Hofmann, D. A. (1999). The structure and function of collective constructs: Implications for multilevel research and theory development. *Academy of Management Review, 24* (2), 249–265.

Norman, D. A. (1993). *Things that make us smart: Defending human attributes in the age of the machine.* Reading, MA: Addison-Wesley.

Norman, D. A. (1998). *The invisible computer: Why good products can fail, the personal computer is so complex, and information appliances are the solution.* Cambridge, MA: MIT Press.

Orlikowski, W. J. (1992). The duality of technology: Rethinking the concept of technology in organizations. *Organization Science, 3* (3), 398–427.

Orlikowski, W. J., Yates, J., Okamura, K., & Fujimoto, M. (1995). Shaping electronic communication: The metastructuring of technology in the context of use. *Organization Science, 6* (4), 423–444.

Osterman, P. (1994). How common is workplace transformation and who adopts it? *Industrial and Labor Relations Review, 47* (2), 173–188.

Parker, S., & Wall, T. (1998). *Job and work design: Organizing work to promote well-being and effectiveness.* Thousand Oaks, CA: Sage.

Parker, S., Wall, T., & Jackson, P. R. (1997). "That's not my job": Developing flexible employee work orientations. *Academy of Management Journal, 40* (4), 899–929.

Pasmore, W., Francis, C. Haldeman, J., & Shani, A. (1982). Sociotechnical systems: A North American reflection on empirical studies of the seventies. *Human Relations, 35,* 1179–1204.

Potter, E. E. (2003). Telecommuting: The future of work, corporate culture, and American society. *Journal of Labor Research, 24* (1), 73–84.

Powell, W. (1990). Neither market nor hierarchy: Network forms of organization. In B. Staw & L. Cummings (Eds.), *Research in organizational behavior, 12* (pp. 295–336). Greenwich, CT: JAI Press.

Pugh, D. S., Hickson, D. J., Hinings, C. R., & Turner, C. (1969). The context of organization structures. *Administrative Science Quarterly, 14,* 91–114.

Raghuram, S., Garud, R., Wiesenfeld, B., & Gupta, V. (2001). Factors contributing to virtual work adjustment. *Journal of Management, 27* (3), 383–405.

Rashford, N. S., & Coghlan, D. (1994). *The dynamics of organizational levels.* Reading, MA: Addison-Wesley.

Reese, R. (1995). Redesigning for dial tone: A sociotechnical systems case study. *Organizational Dynamics, 24,* 80–90.

Renn, R. W., & Vandenburg, R. J. (1995). The critical psychological states: An underrepresented component in job characteristics model research. *Journal of Management, 21* (2), 279–303.

Rice, A. K. (1953). Productivity and social organization in an Indian weaving shed: An examination of some aspects of the sociotechnical system of an experimental automatic loom shed. *Human Relations, 6,* 297–329.

Rice, A. K. (1958). *Productivity and social organization: The Ahmedabad experiments.* London: Tavistock.

Rummler, G. A., & Brache, A. P. (1995). *Improving performance: How to manage the white space on the organization chart* (2nd ed.). San Francisco: Jossey-Bass.

Salvendy, G., & Karwowski, W. (1994). *Design of work and development of personnel in advanced manufacturing.* New York: Wiley-Interscience.

Schick, A. G., Gordon, L. A., & Haka, S. (1990). Information overload: A temporal approach. *Accounting, Organization and Society, 15,* 199–220.

Schoonhoven, C. B. (1981). Problems with contingency theory: Testing assumptions hidden within the language of contingency "theory." *Administrative Science Quarterly, 26,* 349–377.

Scribner, S. (1984). Studying working intelligence. In B. Rogoff & J. Lave (Eds.), *Everyday cognition: Its development in social context.* Cambridge, MA: Harvard University Press.

Semler, S. (1997). Systematic agreement: A theory of organizational alignment. *Human Resource Development Quarterly, 8* (1), 23–40.

Shetty, Y. K. (1986). Quality, productivity, and profit performance: Learning from research and practice. *National Productivity Review, 5* (2), 166–173.

Shewhart, W. A. (1931). *The economic control of manufactured products.* New York: Van Nostrand.

Smith, V. (1997). New forms of work organization. *Annual Review of Sociology, 23,* 315–339.

Staw, B. M., & Boettger, R. D. (1990). Task revision: A neglected form of work performance. *Academy of Management Journal, 33* (3), 534–559.

Tenner, E. (1996). *Why things bite back: Technology and the revenge of unintended consequences.* New York: Knopf.

Thorsrud, D. E. (1968). Sociotechnical approach to job design and organization development. *Management International Review, 8* (4–5), 120–131.

Torraco, R. J. (2000). The relationship of learning and performance improvement at different system levels. *Performance Improvement Quarterly, 13* (1), 60–83.

Torraco, R. J. (2002). Cognitive demands of new technologies and the implications for learning theory. *Human Resource Development Review, 1,* 439–467.

Tracey, J. B., Tannenbaum, S. I., & Kavanaugh, M. J. (1995). Applying trained skills of the job: The importance of the work environment. *Journal of Applied Psychology, 80,* 239–252.

Trist, E. L. (1981). *The evolution of sociotechnical systems.* Toronto: Ontario Quality of Work Life Centre.

Trist, E. L., & Bamforth, K. W. (1951). Some social and psychological consequences of long-wall methods of coal getting. *Human Relations, 4,* 3–38.

Trist, E. L., Higgin, G. W., Murray, H., & Pollock, A. B. (1963). *Organizational choice.* London: Tavistock.

Turnbull, S. (2002). Social construction research and theory building. *Advances in Developing Human Resources, 4,* 317–334.

Tushman, M., & Romanelli, E. (1985). Organizational evolution: A metamorphosis model of convergence and reorientation. In L. L. Cummings & B. M. Staw (Eds.), *Research in organization behavior* (Vol. 7, pp. 171–222). Greenwich, CT: JAI Press.

Venkatesh, V., & Johnson, P. (2002). Telecommuting technology implementations: A within- and between-subjects longitudinal field study. *Personnel Psychology, 55* (3), 661–687.

Volberda, H. W. (1998). Toward the flexible form: How to remain vital in hypercompetitive environments. In A. Y. Ilinitch, A. Lewin, & R. D'Aveni (Eds.), *Managing in times of disorder: Hypercompetitive organizational responses* (pp. 267–296). Thousand Oaks, CA: Sage.

Vygotsky, L. S. (1978). *Mind and society: The development of higher psychological processes.* Cambridge, MA: Harvard University Press.

Watad, M. M., & DiSanzo, F. J. (2000). The synergism of telecommuting and office automation. *Sloan Management Review, 41* (2), 85–96.

Weick, K. A. (1990). Technology as equivoque: Sensemaking in new technologies. In P. S. Goodman, L. S. Sproull, & Associates (Eds.), *Technology and organizations.* San Francisco: Jossey-Bass.

Welsh, D.H.B., Luthans, F., & Sommer, S. M. (1993, February). Managing Russian factory workers: The impact of U.S.-based behavioral and participative techniques. *Academy of Management Journal,* 58–79.

Wognum, I.A.M. (2000). Vertical integration of HRD within companies. In K. P. Kuchinke (Ed.), *Academy of Human Resource Development Conference Proceedings* (pp. 1083–1090). Baton Rouge, LA: AHRD.

Wrzesniewski, A., & Dutton, J. E. (2001). Crafting a job: Revisioning employees as active crafters of their work. *Academy of Management Review, 26* (2), 179–201.

Zucker, L. G. (1987). Institutional theories of organizations. In W. R. Scott (Ed.), *Annual review of sociology* (pp. 443–464). Palo Alto, CA: Annual Reviews.

*Richard J. Torraco is associate professor and coordinator of the graduate program in human resource development, Department of Educational Administration, University of Nebraska.*

# General and Specific Self-Efficacy in the Context of a Training Intervention to Enhance Performance Expectancy

*Catherine E. Schwoerer, Douglas R. May,*
*Elaine C. Hollensbe, Jennifer Mencl*

*A pretest-posttest field study investigated self-efficacy, both general and specific, in an intensive training experience to prepare new recruits for their work assignments. Specific issues addressed include (1) the effects of the training experience on general self-efficacy (GSE), work-specific self-efficacy (SSE), and performance expectancy; (2) the effects of pretraining attitudes and beliefs on posttraining GSE and work SSE; and relations between posttraining self-efficacy beliefs and posttraining performance expectancy. Training increased GSE, SSE, and performance expectancy. Unlike GSE, work SSE was influenced by pretraining motivation, training self-efficacy, and performance expectancy. The implications of the findings for HRD research and practice are discussed from the perspectives of understanding individual characteristics of trainees, choosing methods to enhance self-efficacy, and the appropriateness of measuring general and specific self-efficacy before training (to guide planning) and after training (as an evaluation dimension).*

In recent years, research focusing on antecedent or pretraining influences on subsequent training outcomes and effectiveness has increased significantly. A key antecedent category is the individual characteristics of trainees, or what trainees bring to the training setting (Mathieu, Tannenbaum, & Salas, 1992; Noe, 1986; Noe & Ford, 1992; Salas & Cannon-Bowers, 2001). The wide range

*Note:* We thank the sponsoring organization and the study participants. An earlier version of this article was presented at the Midwest Academy of Management in Kansas City, Missouri. The research was partially supported by a grant from the General Research Fund of the University of Kansas.

of individual characteristics found to predict training motivation and outcomes includes locus of control, conscientiousness, anxiety, age, cognitive ability, job involvement, and self-efficacy (Colquitt, LePine, & Noe, 2000). The recognition of these factors challenges human resource development (HRD) professionals to use this knowledge to enhance training design, delivery, and evaluation. The individual difference of self-efficacy is notable for its relevance in HRD theory, research, and practice (Gibson, 2004). It has been applied to employee learning and development, as well as a number of other HRD topics.

Self-efficacy, which is defined as the belief that one can perform specific tasks and behaviors, has been found to be a robust predictor of learning in training and performance in a wide range of situations (Gist, Schwoerer, & Rosen, 1989; Stajkovic & Luthans, 1998; Tracey, Hinkin, Tannenbaum, & Mathieu, 2001). As a central construct of social cognitive or social learning theory, it offers a relatively comprehensive framework for understanding human learning and behavior (Bandura, 1986). Social learning theory represents learning as a dynamic process of interplay among the person, behavior, and the environment that involves forethought, action, and self-reflection (Bandura, 2001). Congruent with the psychological theory proposed by Swanson (2001), social cognitive theory is one of the three core theories supporting the discipline of HRD.

Within the framework of social cognitive theory, self-efficacy can be conceptualized as relevant before, during, and after training. The study described here examines self-efficacy as both a target of training and as a desirable outcome of training, addressing a need described in the literature (Salas & Cannon-Bowers, 2001). The study also explores the relations among relatively general and specific levels of self-efficacy in order to understand how self-efficacy beliefs are affected by training and how they both serve as training outcomes and predict other significant training outcomes.

Training efforts and programs naturally vary widely in scope and emphasis in a way that complicates the designation of self-efficacy as task specific. While some training focuses on specific skill development (for example, to perform a task), organizations also invest in more comprehensive, broadly targeted training to prepare participants for a range of experiences. This type of training may also serve to build motivation that supports the performance of certain task skills under challenging conditions such as independence or distance from the organization or in situations that require persistence and resilience. Self-efficacy, then, can be developed at differing degrees of task specificity. Some work even suggests that considering an individual's general self-efficacy can be useful (Sherer et al., 1982). Because self-efficacy is a key component in performance, designing training to build self-efficacy at relatively specific and more general levels of specificity offers the potential to enhance current performance. Attending to self-efficacy in training also may enhance trainees' capacity to perform effectively in the future, consistent with a key assumption of HRD's performance paradigm as developed by Holton (2002).

The study described here contributes to the literatures of training and self-efficacy by examining the relative influences of general self-efficacy (GSE) and specific self-efficacy (SSE) on the outcomes of a training program (such as performance expectancy). The training program used a wide range of methods consistent with the principles of enhancing self-efficacy defined by Bandura (1986) in social cognitive theory. This study also investigates the interrelations of GSE and SSE and their malleability in training. These issues are examined in the organizational context of an intensive training intervention designed to prepare participants to cope and work independently as salespeople in dispersed work locations.

## Theoretical Background and Hypotheses

The research described here investigates the influences of both the training intervention and individual trainee characteristics (including demographics, pretraining self-efficacy beliefs, and other pretraining attitudes) on posttraining self-efficacy and performance expectancy. Posttraining self-efficacy is conceptualized as an influence on the awareness and acceptance of performance expectations communicated in training (performance expectancy). This acceptance of performance expectations after training, in combination with a belief in ability to perform, is expected to help trainees cope with their work situations.

*General and Specific Self-Efficacy Beliefs.* Since the late 1980s (Gist, 1987), self-efficacy has received increasing attention from organizational researchers. Research on self-efficacy, or the belief in one's ability to perform a given task (Bandura, 1986, 1997), has generally supported positive relations between efficacy and a range of performance measures and outcomes (see Gist & Mitchell, 1992, for a summary; Stajkovic & Luthans, 1998, for a meta-analysis). Self-efficacy is relevant to understanding training effectiveness since its enhancement through training can increase performance (Gist et al., 1989; Karl, O'Leary-Kelly, & Martocchio, 1993) and help newcomers adapt to their work (Saks, 1995). There is some evidence supporting the utility of including self-efficacy as a basic training evaluation criterion; training that results in high self-efficacy beliefs is more likely to lead to desired posttraining outcomes (Martocchio & Hertenstein, 2003).

Refinements in self-efficacy research have included debate and investigation of the nature of appropriate measurement (Eden & Zuk, 1995; Gist & Mitchell, 1992; Lent & Hackett, 1987; Maurer & Pierce, 1998), including the appropriate degree of specificity in conceptualization and operationalization (Maurer, 2001). While self-efficacy itself is inherently task specific, the specificity of self-efficacy with respect to a given task varies.

This issue of task definition and the appropriate specification of self-efficacy is a key one. For example, an HRD professional interested in how self-efficacy influences learning computer skills that will strengthen performance might identify varying degrees of relevant specificity. General computer use, or feelings of self-efficacy in basic computer operation, might be relevant in some cases and be necessary as a foundation. A focus on more task-specific efficacy beliefs, such as learning software or undertaking programming, might be more relevant in other situations. Thus, relatively general or specific domains are possible within a given task, skill, or behavior.

As the conceptualization of self-efficacy becomes more general, one moves toward the individual differences construct of GSE, a general belief in one's ability to succeed (Sherer et al., 1982). GSE has been investigated as an influence on focused behavioral outcomes, in a manner similar to SSE. For example, Eden and Aviram (1993) studied the impact of GSE on the intensity of job search behavior. Research does not often explicitly recognize both GSE and SSE or generally investigate their relations or their relative contribution to understanding behaviors and outcomes. This compounds the challenge of learning more about how self-efficacy is influenced and how it influences behavior.

Gist and Mitchell (1992) distinguish between self-efficacy and self-esteem but do not address the issue of specificity. They do identify unresolved issues such as influences on self-efficacy and its malleability. Mathieu, Martineau, and Tannenbaum (1993), investigating individual and situational influences on the development of self-efficacy in a bowling class, noted that self-efficacy levels are likely to "exhibit some consistency" (p. 129) and a degree of stability, but that they are also somewhat malleable.

Eden (1988) viewed GSE as a stable traitlike characteristic and SSE as a relatively malleable independent variable. Consistent with this, Eden and Kinnar (1991) investigated GSE as an individual difference and moderator of training effects; SSE served as a manipulation check for comparing training programs expected to be differentially effective in increasing volunteering.

Eden and Aviram (1993) found that GSE was malleable. In their study, those who were unemployed and low in GSE benefited most from the intervention, increasing their job search activities and likelihood of reemployment. Still, relatively little work has compared the utility of general and specific measures or their respective malleability. Indeed, Eden (1988) has recommended using both SSE and GSE in research. One recent study used GSE as a control variable (Davis, Fedor, Parsons, & Herold, 2000). This study contributes further to this area by examining the relative influence and malleability of both GSE and SSE in a training intervention.

The training intervention studied in this research was designed to equip participants for the specific challenges they would face in their work by enhancing their perceptions of control and resilience as well as teaching skills. The training included components that were consistent with theoretical cues to build self-efficacy (Bandura, 1986). These included role plays to provide an experience of success (enactive mastery), models of performance (vicarious experience), coaching and encouragement (verbal persuasion), and reducing the emotional threat of rejection (managing physiological states). Thus, posttraining work SSE (belief in the ability to fulfill specific work requirements) was expected to be directly enhanced by the training.

Sherer et al. (1982) describe their GSE scale as a measure not tied to specific situations or behavior, but built on past experiences with success and failure in a variety of situations. Although it might be influenced, it is conceived as a dispositional measure. Given the relatively short duration of the training intervention studied here and its focus on practicing specific tasks, the training was not expected to influence GSE. Given the above discussion of differences in GSE and SSE beliefs, we propose the following hypothesis:

HYPOTHESIS 1a. *Training experiences and learning will result in increased work SSE.*

HYPOTHESIS 1b. *Training experiences and learning will not affect GSE.*

***Performance Expectancy and Training.*** Performance expectancy refers to the acceptance of and intention to meet performance expectations or goals. Recent work has addressed its theoretical antecedents and its distinctiveness from goal commitment (DeShon & Landis, 1997). Whereas goal commitment has been defined as "one's attachment to or determination to reach a goal" (Locke, Latham, & Erez, 1988, p. 24), performance expectancy is viewed as an antecedent to goal commitment and not a component of the goal commitment construct itself (DeShon & Landis, 1997).

Performance expectancy is not interchangeable with self-efficacy and goals because it is defined as a cognitive intention. An intention is defined by Tubbs and Ekeberg (1991) as a cognitive representation of both the objective one is striving for and the action plan one intends to use to reach that objective. Thus, an intention is a broad and inclusive concept that is particularly relevant as an outcome of a training intervention designed to equip participants with the information and skills they will need to perform in a subsequent setting. Self-efficacy refers not to the intention of performance expectancy but the beliefs that an individual has that he or she can successfully carry out the actions necessary to accomplish intentions.

Tan, Hall, and Boyce (2003), in a study examining cognitive and affective reactions to a training intervention, drew on Ajzen's theory of planned behavior (1991) as support in discussing the relevance of cognitive reactions to training as indicators of subsequent on-the-job performance. Indeed, Gellatly (1996) found that performance expectancy played a mediating role between conscientiousness and task performance. Training, which increases experience with the relevant tasks and can enhance self-efficacy, is expected to result in greater acceptance or intention to undertake the necessary action steps to meet performance goals. Performance expectancy, then, is a precursor and guide to performance outcomes. This discussion leads to the following hypothesis:

HYPOTHESIS 1c. *Training experiences and learning will result in increased performance expectancy.*

*Pretraining Beliefs and Attitudes.* In addition to the learning and experiences embedded in and provided by training itself, trainees' attitudes and beliefs influence training outcomes; these are among the individual characteristics that constitute what trainees bring to the training setting (Noe, 1986; Salas & Cannon-Bowers, 2001). The following sections address additional influences on posttraining self-efficacy and performance expectancy.

*Training Specific Self-Efficacy.* Training SSE refers to an individual's belief in his or her ability to learn and succeed in training (Guthrie & Schwoerer, 1994). It can be viewed as a prerequisite for taking advantage of training. If one perceives a high likelihood of succeeding in training, one is better prepared for and more positive about the experience. Guthrie and Schwoerer (1994) have found that training SSE was linked to perceptions of training utility or views of training as helpful or instrumental. Confidence in one's ability to succeed at training (prior to the beginning of the training experience) is associated with positive expectations about the experience. These positive expectations likely create a greater sense of openness and thus enhance the self-efficacy one feels at training's end.

*Training Motivation.* Trainee motivation to learn the content of a training program and transfer that knowledge to the work setting was also proposed by Noe (1986) as an influence on learning and behavior. Mathieu et al. (1992) found that training motivation was weakly linked to learning and more strongly associated with reactions to training. Baldwin and Ford (1988) proposed a model of the transfer process that includes trainee motivation as a training input that can influence training outcomes and facilitate transfer. Although this study does not directly address transfer, it does assess posttraining outcomes such as work SSE that can be expected to influence posttraining behaviors, including the transfer of newly learned skills to work. In a meta-analysis, Colquitt et al. (2000) found motivation to learn explained significant variance in knowledge declaration, skill acquisition, posttraining self-efficacy, and reactions to training above and beyond cognitive ability. Training motivation is expected to create greater openness to training, facilitating the development of work SSE, and resulting ultimately in effective transfer and enhanced work performance.

*Performance Expectancy.* As an individual begins training, he or she has some sense of buy-in to the purposes of that training: a degree of intention to invest effort and meet training expectations and goals. This preliminary attachment, in combination with the opportunity and motivation to experience success and build work SSE in training, can be expected to influence performance expectancy at the conclusion of training. Posttraining work SSE, or strengthened belief in ability to perform the tasks necessary to accomplish work, can be reasonably expected to help a training participant view the goals involved in doing work as more manageable. Specifically, it can lead the trainee to hold the intention to meet performance expectations (that is, increase performance expectancy) and provide a supportive antecedent to goal commitment (Klein, Wesson, Hollenbeck, & Alge, 1999). In contrast, GSE perceptions do not directly link to job-specific beliefs, behaviors, or goals.

The pretraining cognitions of training SSE, training motivation, and performance expectancy are believed to influence posttraining SSE but not GSE. Because these cognitions are directly related to training, they are likely to influence the experience of training and, in turn, posttraining SSE. In contrast, GSE, a general outlook reflecting varied, numerous experiences of success over an extended period (Sherer et al., 1982), is not expected to change significantly in a brief period or to be highly susceptible to these situation-specific cognitions. Based on the preceding discussion, the following hypotheses are proposed:

HYPOTHESIS 2a. *Pretraining cognitions (training SSE, training motivation, and performance expectancy) will positively influence work SSE at training's end.*

HYPOTHESIS 2b. *Pretraining cognitions (training SSE, training motivation, and performance expectancy) will not influence GSE at training's end.*

HYPOTHESIS 3. *Posttraining work SSE, but not posttraining GSE, will positively influence performance expectancy at training's end.*

## Method

A field study of individuals hired for summer work in independent, door-to-door contractor sales of family-oriented educational reference books and software was conducted.

***Research Design and Procedure.*** Individuals who participated in the program represent over three hundred colleges and universities in the United States. In preparation for assigning recently hired recruits, the large U.S. company provided an intensive five-day training workshop. The program included motivational speakers, videos, simulations, and role play, including modeling followed by practice and feedback, experiences that Bandura (1986) proposed to influence the development of self-efficacy. Specifically, the training introduced individuals to the basic principles of sales success, sales theory, and sales techniques. The history of selling was emphasized along with the salesperson's role in today's society. The sales course applied communication theory and principles to the sales situation. The history and philosophy of the company as an example of a successful sales organization was also presented.

On the first day, before training began (Time 1, or T1), an administrative assistant in the company distributed and collected a survey that assessed GSE, training SSE, work SSE, performance expectancy, and training motivation, as well as demographic data. The second survey, administered at the end of the training period on the fifth day (Time 2, or T2), assessed posttraining GSE, work SSE, and performance expectancy. Cook and Campbell (1979) categorize this as a one-group, pretest-posttest design. Both questionnaires included a brief description of the nature and purpose of the research. Instructions stated that the voluntary questionnaire was part of a study to "understand more about the work-related attitudes and training activities of salespeople." Instructions emphasized that individual responses would be confidential and that only summaries would be provided to management. The same survey administrator gave participants approximately fifteen minutes to complete the survey and attempted to answer all questions consistently across group administrations.

*Participants.* Of the 558 sales representatives participating in the training workshop, 485 (87 percent) completed the T1 questionnaire and 492 (88 percent) completed the T2 questionnaire. Questionnaires from the two time periods were cross-matched on identification numbers to obtain 420 matched pairs as the final subject number, for a final response rate of 75 percent.

The mean age of participants was twenty years, and the mean year in college was 2.8 (closest to the junior year). Sixty percent were male. The mean grade point average (GPA) reported was 3.1 on a four-point scale. Twelve percent of the participants would work as sales managers, providing support to those without experience, in addition to selling.

*Setting.* The employees attended the week-long training session at a central location and then moved to their assigned sales regions located throughout several states. Salespeople worked independently on a contract basis; they bought products at wholesale and sold them at retail. The training included realistic practice in giving product demonstrations. Participants were encouraged to set and achieve performance goals to give a specific number of these product demonstrations weekly in their region.

*Measures.* The study encompassed a number of measures.

*General Self-Efficacy.* GSE was measured at both time periods using the seventeen items developed by Sherer et al. (1982) and a seven-point Likert scale. Internal scale reliability for all measures was determined using Cronbach's alpha. The alpha results for the GSE scale were very similar to Sherer et al.'s result (1982) of .86 (T1 alpha = .87; T2 = .88). Sample statements measuring general self-efficacy include: "When I make plans, I am certain I can make them work" and "If something looks too complicated, I will not even bother to try it" (reverse coded).

*Work-Specific Self-Efficacy.* Work SSE was measured before and after training using twelve items on a seven-point Likert scale (T1 alpha = .89; T2 = .85). The participants were asked to indicate the extent to which they were confident in their ability to "handle rejection; stay motivated; approach people to make a presentation; make a sales presentation, fill out sales records," and others. The items were developed using the company's description of the skills and capabilities necessary to succeed in the sales role. Such an approach is consistent with previous research in this area (Frayne & Geringer, 2000).

*Performance Expectancy.* Performance expectancy refers to the individual's intention to meet performance expectations. In this study, these intentions referred to the number of demonstrations given and hours worked. Both are seen by company officials as key predictors of success and performance in the posttraining assignment. Performance expectancy was measured before and after training with four seven-point Likert-scale items (T1 alpha = .83; T2 = .77). A sample performance expectancy item is, "I will strive to attain the goal of working 80 hours per week."

*Training Self-Efficacy and Training Motivation.* Training SSE and training motivation were measured at Time 1. *Training SSE* refers to the belief in one's capability to perform successfully in training and was measured with a six-item scale (alpha = .84) used by Guthrie and Schwoerer (1994). A sample item is, "I am confident that I can succeed in training." *Training motivation* was measured using four items (sample item: "I will try to learn as much as I can from the training program") on a seven-point Likert scale (alpha = .77).

*Demographic Variables.* Demographic variables that might influence reactions to training were measured and controlled for statistically in the analysis: gender (0 = female; 1 = male), cumulative grade point average (four-point scale), and whether a respondent was a sales manager (0 = yes; 1 = no), indicating previous experience. These self-reported data were included in the study and analysis to increase confidence in the findings for the variables of central interest to the study. Demographics are rarely the focus of empirical research on training, and there is little theory linking demographics to training outcomes. However, their control can clarify the relations among other variables.

Although the results for gender on learning are equivocal (Colquitt et al., 2000), there is research evidence suggesting that females and males differ in their achievement-related self-confidence and their performance expectancies in entrepreneurial conditions (Gatewood, Shaver, Powers & Gartner, 2002). Given the focus on general and specific self-efficacy as well as performance expectancies in this study, we chose to control for gender.

General cognitive ability and prior job knowledge are also established as predictors of self-efficacy, job knowledge, and performance in training (Ree, Carretta, & Teachout, 1995; Colquitt et al., 2000). In the organization studied, the sales manager designation is a proxy for experience, since recruits in this role all had previous success in the focal job. Grade point average is used widely in recruiting and believed to capture the work-related constructs of cognitive ability and motivation (Roth & Bobko, 2000); thus, it is a useful proxy for general cognitive ability and pretraining motivation.

*Data Analyses.* Paired comparison *t*-tests were used to assess the T1 to T2 changes in GSE, SSE, and performance expectancy (hypotheses 1a, 1b, and 1c). Hierarchical regression analyses were used to determine support for the hypotheses investigating the effect of T1 measures on T2 measures (hypotheses 2a, 2b, and 3). Analyses controlled for demographics and the value of relevant T1 variables by entering these control measures in separate steps. This analytical method isolates the effects attributable to these variables and assesses the incremental variance explained by subsequent variables.

## Results

Here we examine the relations among the variables, the effects of training, postttraining general and specific self-efficacy, and influences on posttraining performance expectancy.

*Relations Among the Variables.* Means, standard deviations, and correlations among the study variables are provided in Table 1. Consistent with the company's systematic selection for individuals with sales potential, investigations revealed that performance expectancy, general self-efficacy, training motivation, and training self-efficacy were all somewhat negatively skewed at Time 1. Work specific self-efficacy was slightly positively skewed at Time 1 and became negatively skewed at Time 2, after the training. Study variables also tended to have somewhat tall distributions. Any outliers were included in the analyses.

Results indicate that T1 and T2 measures of general self-efficacy are highly correlated; it appears that general self-efficacy did not change greatly during the training period. In contrast, the correlations between work SSE and performance expectancy at T1 and T2 are relatively smaller.

Demographic variables were not highly correlated with the T2 variables, although GPA was correlated with training motivation and performance expectancy at T1. Those holding the position of sales manager reported higher pretraining training motivation, training self-efficacy, and work-specific self-efficacy going into the training, probably due to their previous successful experience. Since significant correlations existed among some of the dependent measures, supplementary principal components factor analyses with varimax rotation were conducted on the three dependent variables (general self-efficacy, work-specific self-efficacy, and performance expectancy) at both T1 and T2. All scale items loaded on the appropriate specified factor, with only one item cross-loading above .40 at either time period. Eigenvalues for the three factors ranged from 2.6 to 7.3 at Time 1 and from 2.3 to 8.4 at Time 2. In sum, the findings of the factor analysis reinforce the theoretical and empirical discriminant validities of the dependent variables.

*Effects of Training.* The results of the paired comparison *t*-tests used to test hypotheses 1a, 1b, and 1c are summarized in Table 2. Consistent with the hypothesis, both work-specific self-efficacy and performance expectancy increased after training. Contrary to expectations, general self-efficacy increased significantly. Participants' work-specific self-efficacy appears to be more affected by the training (T1 mean = 3.74; T2 mean = 6.26).

*Posttraining General and Specific Self-Efficacy.* Hierarchical regression analyses were used to assess the effects of T1 measures on general self-efficacy and work-specific self-efficacy at T2 proposed in hypotheses 2a and 2b (see Table 3). Results provide general support for the hypotheses. T2 general self-efficacy was significantly influenced only by T1 general self-efficacy. In contrast, T2 work-specific self-efficacy was positively influenced by T1 measures of

**Table 1. Means, Standard Deviations, and Intercorrelations Among Study Variables**

| Variable | Mean | SD | 1 | 2 | 3 | 4 | 5 | 6 | 7 | 8 | 9 | 10 | 11 |
|---|---|---|---|---|---|---|---|---|---|---|---|---|---|
| 1. Gender | .59 | .49 | — | | | | | | | | | | |
| 2. GPA | 3.07 | .49 | -.20 | — | | | | | | | | | |
| 3. Manager | .88 | .32 | -.06 | .03 | — | | | | | | | | |
| 4. Training Motivation | 6.63 | .43 | -.03 | .13 | -.17 | — | | | | | | | |
| 5. Training SSE | 5.70 | .40 | .03 | .04 | -.11 | .49 | — | | | | | | |
| 6. General Self-Efficacy (T1) | 5.72 | .68 | .02 | .11 | -.02 | .41 | .31 | — | | | | | |
| 7. General Self-Efficacy (T2) | 5.87 | .73 | .02 | .09 | .01 | .31 | .23 | .74 | — | | | | |
| 8. Work-Specific Self-Efficacy (T1) | 3.74 | 1.19 | .08 | -.02 | -.18 | .13 | .07 | .25 | .21 | — | | | |
| 9. Work-Specific Self-Efficacy (T2) | 6.26 | .54 | .03 | -.06 | -.13 | .39 | .36 | .43 | .48 | .17 | — | | |
| 10. Performance Expectancy (T1) | 6.68 | .53 | -.15 | .22 | -.10 | .41 | .24 | .19 | .09 | .03 | .26 | — | |
| 11. Performance Expectancy (T2) | 6.86 | .34 | -.01 | .12 | .05 | .27 | .17 | .17 | .14 | .04 | .29 | .47 | — |

*Note: N* = 386–417, depending on missing data. T1 = Time 1; T2 = Time 2. Correlations: ≥.10 significant at *p* < .05; ≥.13 significant at *p* < .01.

**Table 2. Pre-Post Training Changes in General and Work-Specific Self-Efficacy and Performance Expectancy**

|  | Time 1 Mean (SD) | Time 2 Mean (SD) | t-test |
|---|---|---|---|
| General Self-Efficacy | 5.72 | 5.87 |  |
|  | (.68) | (.72) | 5.78** |
| Work-Specific Self-Efficacy | 3.74 | 6.26 |  |
|  | (1.19) | (.54) | 42.22** |
| Performance Expectancy | 6.68 | 6.87 |  |
|  | (.53) | (.34) | 7.90** |

*$p < .05$. **$p < .01$.

**Table 3. Hierarchical Multiple Regression Results for the Influences on Posttraining Self-Efficacy**

|  | General Self-Efficacy | | Work-Specific Self-Efficacy | |
|---|---|---|---|---|
|  | β | $R^2$ Change | β | $R^2$ Change |
| **Step 1** |  |  |  |  |
| Sex | .00 |  | −.01 |  |
| GPA | .02 |  | −.14** |  |
| Manager Position | .03 |  | −.05 |  |
|  |  | .01 |  | .02 |
| **Step 2** |  |  |  |  |
| General Self-Efficacy (Time 1) | .73** |  | .29** |  |
| Work-Specific Self-Efficacy (Time 1) | .03 |  | .05 |  |
|  |  | .54** |  | .19** |
| **Step 3** |  |  |  |  |
| Training Efficacy | .01 |  | .16** |  |
| Training Motivation | .03 |  | .15** |  |
| Performance Expectancy | −.06 |  | .13** |  |
|  |  | .01 |  | .11** |
| Overall model F |  | 59.17** |  | 20.21** |
| Adjusted $R^2$ |  | .55 |  | .29 |

Note: $N = 384$ for dependent variables due to listwise deletion of missing data. Regression coefficients listed are the standardized beta coefficients at each step of the equation.
*$p < .05$. **$p < .01$.

training SSE, training motivation, and performance expectancy. Interestingly, T1 general self-efficacy was also a significant factor. The block of demographic variables did not explain significant variance in either T2 general self-efficacy or T2 work-specific self-efficacy.

*Influences on Posttraining Performance Expectancy.* Hierarchical regression was used to investigate the influences on posttraining performance expectancy

**Table 4. Hierarchical Multiple Regression Results
for Posttraining Performance Expectancy**

| | Posttraining Performance Expectancy | |
|---|---|---|
| | β | $R^2$ Change |
| Step 1 | | |
| Sex | .04 | |
| GPA | .04 | |
| Manager Position | .15** | .02 |
| Step 2 | | |
| Performance Expectancy (Time 1) | .48** | .54** |
| Step 3 | | |
| General Self-Efficacy (Time 1) | −.04 | |
| Work Specific Self-Efficacy (Time 1) | .03 | .01 |
| Step 4 | | |
| General Self-Efficacy (Time 2) | .02 | |
| Work Specific Self-Efficacy (Time 2) | .20** | .03* |
| Overall model F | 21.52** | |
| Adjusted $R^2$ | .30 | |

*Note:* $N = 385$ for dependent variables due to listwise deletion of missing data. Regression coefficients listed are the standardized beta coefficients at each step of the equation.
*$p < .05$. **$p < .01$.

suggested in hypothesis 3 (see Table 4). Analysis was conducted in several steps, with the following results:

- Demographic variables did not explain a significant amount of variance (step 1).
- Controlling for T1 performance expectancy, significant variance was explained (step 2).
- General self-efficacy and work-specific self-efficacy at T1 were not significant in explaining T2 performance expectancy (step 3).
- General self-efficacy and work-specific self-efficacy at T2 explained a significant amount of additional variance (step 4).

Beta coefficients indicate that work-specific self-efficacy was the significant variable; higher work-specific self-efficacy led to higher final performance expectancy.

## Discussion

Consistent with expectations, this research found that training experiences designed to equip participants to cope independently with a challenging work situation had a positive influence on specific efficacy beliefs (work SSE) and acceptance of and intention to meet performance goals (performance expectancy). Contrary to expectations, the training also influenced their GSE, although it influenced work SSE to a greater extent.

The research revealed that work SSE at the end of training could be explained in part by relevant cognitions (training SSE, training motivation, and initial performance expectancy) brought to the training situation. In contrast, GSE at the conclusion of training was explained best only by initial levels of GSE. Posttraining work SSE beliefs were, in turn, predictors of final performance expectancy, unlike GSE at training's end. The following sections examine how these findings might be integrated into the literature on training and self-efficacy.

*Training Effects on SSE and GSE.* The results of our study suggest that a focus on SSE provides more knowledge about how a training program works than does GSE. While GSE can be adequate to establish links between training programs and outcomes in some cases (Eden & Aviram, 1993), attention to SSE might aid in designing training evaluations and tracking their effectiveness at a detailed level; neglecting it might well be risky. Indeed, Martocchio and Hertenstein (2003) have noted that training that results in high self-efficacy is more likely to lead to positive outcomes. Similarly, the SSE outcomes of the training intervention here also reinforce Gibson's view (2004) of the importance of self-efficacy and social cognitive theory in HRD research and practice.

Consistent with Eden and Aviram (1993), this study found that GSE was somewhat malleable, contrary to our initial expectations. The intensive training experiences and learning that occurred affected the participants' general self-efficacy beliefs. It is possible that such a finding was due to the specific population under study: relatively young, inexperienced salespeople who are still maturing. Perhaps these participants have not had life experience with enough different situations to create the stability that Eden (1988) and Sherer et al. (1982) theorize for GSE. Future research should investigate training effects on GSE among different populations in a variety of situations to tease out whether GSE is the stable, traitlike characteristic that Eden (1988) proposed.

*Performance Expectancy.* Performance expectancy was positively influenced by training experiences in this study. The results suggest that training programs can enhance the cognitive intention to invest effort and meet the expectations established in training. In this case, these included the intentions to meet demanding standards that required persistence and resilience across a period of time. This personal internalization of performance means and ends is theorized to lead to goal commitment (DeShon & Landis, 1997) and higher performance (Wofford, Goodwin, & Premack, 1992).

Final performance expectancy was influenced by work SSE at the end of training but not by GSE. This finding is consistent with research on the relation between efficacy and a range of performance outcomes (Gist & Mitchell, 1992) and extends our knowledge of the differential effects of work SSE and GSE. It may be that in this case, the relationship can be understood from the perspective of intentions. Since work SSE beliefs focus on the specific competency beliefs relating to the skills needed for job performance, they influence the specific intentions to engage in the necessary means to accomplish goals and succeed in the subsequent work assignment (performance expectancy). General efficacy beliefs, or GSE, while enhanced in the training experience, do not influence specific posttraining intentions. Future research should examine links among general and specific efficacy beliefs, performance expectancy, and actual performance outcomes, which earlier research has associated with performance expectancy (Gellatly, 1996).

*Pretraining Beliefs and Attitudes.* The significant role of the pretraining measures of training SSE, training motivation, and performance expectancy suggests the usefulness of considering these in developing training. In this case, initial levels of self-efficacy, motivation, and performance expectancy influenced a key posttraining outcome, work SSE. These variables appear to create a type of psychological readiness for training. This study extends work by Guthrie and Schwoerer (1994), who found that training SSE was related to training utility perceptions, and it reinforces research by Mathieu et al. (1992) and Tracey et al. (2001) that training motivation was related to reactions to training (here, work SSE).

A growing body of research suggests that those initially low in self-efficacy receive significant benefits from interventions that build self-efficacy in the context of training for skills (Eden & Aviram, 1993). In this study, participants had relatively low initial levels of work SSE and high levels of GSE. Increased attention to efficacy levels could improve training effectiveness, as could greater understanding of GSE and SSE as complementary individual characteristics.

Overall, future research should continue to investigate the links among self-efficacy, general and specific, and related cognitions and outcomes, as well as the effect of the situation or environment. Learning environments such as training are a particularly fruitful focus for such interactionist investigations suggested by social cognitive theory (Gibson, 2004). In training, individuals are actively engaging in self-assessment as well as acquiring skill and knowledge and forming intentions regarding the means they will use and the ends they will pursue after training. Understanding and enhancing the effectiveness of these processes also offers the potential for HRD professionals to enhance the systemic influence of development efforts.

*Strengths and Limitations.* The time-lagged design of this study including pre- and posttraining measures offers significant advantages over cross-sectional data-gathering efforts. The one-group, pretest-posttest design also has significant weaknesses. Cook and Campbell (1979) elaborate on these, including the threats of statistical regression, testing, history, and maturation. However, they note that working with relatively short time intervals and relatively novel outcomes can balance some of these weaknesses. The time interval here was reasonably short, and the training was focused and highly structured (with the extensive use of motivational speakers, videos, simulations, modeling, practice, and feedback) and relatively unique for these participants. The design allowed for control of some possibly influential variables, such as previous experience and academic achievement, although demographics appeared to be of little importance.

It is also worth noting that the participating organization's approach to recruiting, selecting, and training these participants is quite systematic. The organization's summer employment opportunities are attractive to those interested in sales careers and well known to recruiters who hire fledgling salespeople after university education. A combination of realistic job previews during initial recruiting and self-selection processes suggests that the participants represent a fairly unique group—highly self-efficacious and motivated. This might limit the variance on some of the pretraining attitudes and amount to a situational constraint as discussed by Peters, O'Connor, and Eulberg (1985). Nonetheless, significant results emerged in the study.

*Implications for HRD Practice.*  Consistent with the foundations of HRD, this study's findings have implications for employee learning and subsequent performance (Holton, 2002). First, the results showed that initial training SSE and training motivation are likely to influence significant training outcomes (such as work SSE). Because orientation training takes place when employees begin new jobs, managers would benefit from selecting employees with high motivation and confidence in learning capability, as well as positive general self-efficacy, in order to increase the likelihood that these individuals will perform well during initial training sessions.

The methods used in the training sessions for this study incorporated tasks enabling employees to learn through mastery experiences, vicarious learning, social persuasion, and psychological arousal (Bandura, 1986). These training elements not only allowed employees to acquire job-specific skills and managerial support but also had a significant effect on increasing employees' work SSE, an important criterion of basic training interventions (Martocchio & Hertenstein, 2003). Therefore, HRD professionals would benefit from designing training activities based on these four methods when this type of self-efficacy is identified as a training outcome criterion.

In addition, the influence of work SSE on performance expectancy informs HRD practice. This finding reinforces previous research that individuals with high self-efficacy set more challenging goals and expectations, which leads to higher performance achievement (Latham, 2000). This suggests that work SSE and performance expectancy should be measured to evaluate the effectiveness of training programs. Not only does this provide information regarding the design of training interventions, but it also provides predictive information on how well employees will likely perform once they are on the job (Tan et al., 2003). If individual performance expectancies are lower than organizational standards, managers have an opportunity to provide employees with immediate feedback. This is especially important in short-term, temporary jobs such as the one in this study.

## References

Ajzen, I. (1991). The theory of planned behavior. *Organizational Behavior and Human Decision Processes, 50,* 179–211.

Baldwin, T. T., & Ford, J. K. (1988). Transfer of training: A review and directions for future research. *Personnel Psychology, 41,* 63–106.

Bandura, A. (1986). *Social foundations of thought and action: A social cognitive theory.* Upper Saddle River, NJ: Prentice Hall.

Bandura, A. (1997). *Self-efficacy: The exercise of control.* New York: Freeman.

Bandura, A. (2001). Social cognitive theory: An agentic perspective. *Annual Review of Psychology, 52,* 1–26.

Colquitt, J. A., LePine, J. A., & Noe, R. A. (2000). Toward an integrative theory of training motivation. *Journal of Applied Psychology, 85,* 678–707.

Cook, T. D., & Campbell, D. T. (1979). *Quasi-experimentation: Design and analysis issues for field settings.* Boston: Houghton Mifflin.

Davis, W. D., Fedor, D. B., Parsons, C. K., & Herold, D. M. (2000). The development of self-efficacy during aviation training. *Journal of Organizational Behavior, 21,* 857–871.

DeShon, R. P., & Landis, R. S. (1997). The dimensionality of the Hollenbeck, Williams, & Klein (1989) measure of goal commitment on complex tasks. *Organizational Behavior and Human Decision Processes, 70,* 105–116.

Eden, D. (1988). Pygmalion, goal setting, and expectancy: Compatible ways to raise productivity. *Academy of Management Review, 13,* 639–652.

Eden, D., & Aviram, A. (1993). Self-efficacy training to speed reemployment: Helping people to help themselves. *Journal of Applied Psychology, 78,* 352–360.

Eden, D., & Kinnar, J. (1991). Modeling Galatea: Boosting self-efficacy to increase volunteering. *Journal of Applied Psychology, 76,* 770–780.

Eden, D., & Zuk, Y. (1995). Seasickness as a self-fulfilling prophecy: Raising self-efficacy to boost performance at sea. *Journal of Applied Psychology, 5,* 628–635.

Frayne, C. A., & Geringer, J. M. (2000). Self-management training for improving job performance: A field experiment involving salespeople. *Journal of Applied Psychology, 85,* 361–372.

Gatewood, E. J., Shaver, K. G., Powers, J. B., & Gartner, W. B. (2002). Entrepreneurial expectancy, task effort, and performance. *Entrepreneurship Theory and Practice, 27,* 95–114.

Gellatly, I. R. (1996). Conscientiousness and task performance: Test of a cognitive process model. *Journal of Applied Psychology, 81,* 474–482.

Gibson, S. K. (2004). Social learning (cognitive) theory and implications for human resource development. *Advances in Developing Human Resources, 6,* 193–210.

Gist, M. E. (1987). Self-efficacy: Implications for organizational behavior and human resource management. *Academy of Management Review, 12,* 472–485.

Gist, M. E., & Mitchell, T. R. (1992). Self-efficacy: A theoretical analysis of its determinants and malleability. *Academy of Management Review, 17,* 183–211.

Gist, M. E., Schwoerer, C. E., & Rosen, B. (1989). Effects of alternative training methods on self-efficacy and performance in computer software training. *Journal of Applied Psychology, 74,* 884–891.

Guthrie, J. P., & Schwoerer, C. E. (1994). Individual and contextual influences on self-assessed training needs. *Journal of Organizational Behavior, 15,* 405–422.

Holton, E. F. (2002). Theoretical assumptions underlying the performance paradigm of human resource development. *Human Resource Development International, 5,* 199–215.

Karl, K. A., O'Leary-Kelly, A., & Martocchio, J. J. (1993). The impact of feedback and self-efficacy on performance in training. *Journal of Organizational Behavior, 14,* 379–394.

Klein, H. J., Wesson, M. J., Hollenbeck, J. R., & Alge, B. J. (1999). Goal commitment and the goal-setting process: Conceptual clarification and empirical synthesis. *Journal of Applied Psychology, 84,* 885–896.

Latham, G. P. (2000). Motivate employee performance through goal-setting. In E. A. Locke (Ed.), *Handbook of principles of organizational behavior* (pp. 107–119). Oxford: Blackwell.

Lent, R. W., & Hackett, G. (1987). Career self-efficacy: Empirical status and future directions, *Journal of Vocational Behavior, 30,* 347–382.

Locke, E. A., Latham, G. P., & Erez, M. (1988). The determinants of goal commitment. *Academy of Management Review, 13,* 23–39.

Martocchio, J. J., & Hertenstein, E. J. (2003). Learning orientation and goal orientation context: Relationships with cognitive and affective learning outcomes. *Human Resource Development Quarterly, 14,* 413–434.

Mathieu, J. E., Martineau, J. W., & Tannenbaum, S. I. (1993). Individual and situational influences on the development of self-efficacy: Implications for training effectiveness. *Personnel Psychology, 46,* 125–147.

Mathieu, J. E., Tannenbaum, S. I., & Salas, E. (1992). Influences of individual and situational characteristics on measures of training effectiveness. *Academy of Management Journal, 35,* 828–847.

Maurer, T. J. (2001). Career-relevant learning and development, worker age, and beliefs about self-efficacy for development. *Journal of Management, 27,* 123–140.

Maurer, T. J., & Pierce, H. R. (1998). A comparison of Likert scale and traditional measures of self-efficacy. *Journal of Applied Psychology, 83,* 324–329.

Noe, R. A. (1986). Trainees' attributes and attitudes: Neglected influences on training effectiveness. *Academy of Management Review, 11,* 736–749.

Noe, R. A., & Ford, J. K. (1992). Emerging issues and new directions for training research. In K. M. Rowland & G. Ferris (Eds.), *Research in personnel and human resources management* (Vol. 10, pp. 345–384). Greenwich, CT: JAI Press.

Peters, L. H., O'Connor, E. J., & Eulberg, J. R. (1985). Situational constraints: Sources, consequences, and future considerations. In K. M. Rowland & G. Ferris (Eds.), *Research in personnel and human resources management* (Vol. 3, pp. 79–114). Greenwich, CT: JAI Press.

Ree, M. J., Carretta, T. R., & Teachout, M. S. (1995). Role of ability and prior job knowledge in complex training performance. *Journal of Applied Psychology, 80,* 721–730.

Roth, P. L., & Bobko, P. (2000). College grade point average as a personnel selection device: Ethnic group differences and potential adverse impact. *Journal of Applied Psychology, 85,* 399–406.

Saks, A. M. (1995). Longitudinal field investigation of the moderating and mediating effects of self-efficacy on the relationship between training and newcomer adjustment. *Journal of Applied Psychology, 80,* 211–225.

Salas, E., & Cannon-Bowers, J. A. (2001). The science of training: A decade of progress. *Annual Review of Psychology, 52,* 471–499.

Sherer, M., Maddux, J. E., Mercadente, B., Prentice-Dunn, S., Jacobs, B., & Rogers, R. W. (1982). The self-efficacy scale: Construction and validation. *Psychological Reports, 51,* 663–671.

Stajkovic, A. D., & Luthans, F. (1998). Self-efficacy and work-related performance: A meta-analysis. *Psychological Bulletin, 124,* 240–261.

Swanson, R. A. (2001). Human resource development and its underlying theory. *Human Resource Development International, 4,* 299–312.

Tan, J. A., Hall, R. J., & Boyce, C. (2003). The role of employee reactions in predicting training effectiveness. *Human Resource Development Quarterly, 14,* 397–411.

Tracey, J. B., Hinkin, T. R., Tannenbaum, S., & Mathieu, J. E. (2001). The influence of individual characteristics and the work environment on varying levels of training outcomes. *Human Resource Development Quarterly, 12,* 5–23.

Tubbs, M. E., & Ekeberg, S. E. (1991). The role of intentions in work motivation: Implications for goal-setting theory and research. *Academy of Management Review, 16,* 180–199.

Wofford, J. C., Goodwin, V. L., & Premack, S. (1992). Meta-analysis of the antecedents of personal goal level and of the antecedents and consequences of goal commitment. *Journal of Management, 18,* 595–615.

*Catherine E. Schwoerer is associate professor in the School of Business at the University of Kansas in Lawrence.*

*Douglas R. May is associate professor and director of the Program in Business, Ethics, and Society, Department of Management, at the University of Nebraska-Lincoln.*

*Elaine C. Hollensbe is assistant professor in the Department of Management at the University of Cincinnati in Ohio.*

*Jennifer Mencl is assistant professor in the Department of Management Studies at the University of Minnesota Duluth.*

For bulk reprints of this article, please call (201) 748-8789.

# Why Humanistic Approaches in HRD Won't Work

*David McGuire, Christine Cross, David O'Donnell*

*Humanism has long been considered a cherished worldview underpinning human resource development. As such, it occupies a privileged status within the field, and in the main, its central tenets have gone unchallenged, despite massive changes in the economic, sociological, and technological structure of work and society. This article challenges the preeminence of humanism and argues that the rhetoric of humanistic approaches is not matched by organizational actions of compressed career progression pathways, tight budgetary constraints, and a market-driven economic philosophy.*

In recent years, we have been subjected to a vast range of articles advancing a humanistic value-based approach to human resource development (HRD). This weight of evidence supposedly signals a transition to a more employee-centered form of management practice. The perceived effectiveness of this approach to HRD rests on the assumption that meeting job-related personal needs will lead to employees' moving from job compliance to job commitment. Employees are encouraged to develop personal relationships with the organization, and the message delivered from the upper echelons is that their contributions to the organization are recognized, valued and rewarded.

Aktouf (1992) maintains that humanistic approaches can effectively transform the passive-obedient Taylorist employee into an active-cooperative one. There is some evidence to support the economics of this position. In a seminal study, Huselid (1995) empirically identifies an organization's culture as exhibiting a significant impact on a firm's long-term economic performance; Schuster (1998) finds that employee-centered management practices have the potential to create significant improvements in organizational performance; and in an analysis of *Fortune's* "100 Best Companies to Work for in America," Fulmer, Gerhart, and Scott (2003) present further evidence of links between

*Note:* David McGuire acknowledges the financial support of the Irish American Fulbright Commission.

positive employee relations and performance as measured by accounting and market data.

Notwithstanding the perceived benefits of humanistic approaches, this article argues that humanistic approaches are fundamentally misguided because they fail to fully grasp, take account of, or make explicit the core principles that continue to underpin the capitalist enterprise. Humanism does not change the fundamental laws of economics. We examine some of the key assumptions underpinning humanistic approaches and touch on some of the ethical obligations suggested for HRD practitioners.

## Core Assumptions of Humanistic Approaches

Without question, human resources are a key element in the operation of organizational systems and are central to organizational effectiveness (Kruger, 1998). The transition from rigid bureaucratic structures to more flexible adaptive organizations has been accompanied by some shift in management styles from hierarchical traditions to more human relations–oriented expertise (Henderson, 1996). Humanistic approaches in HRD trace their roots to the field of humanistic psychology, particularly the work of Carl Rogers and the early human relations school, emphasizing the importance of self-esteem and self-development to employee workplace performance (Knowles, Holton, & Swanson, 1998; Addesso, 1996). Such approaches are grounded in the belief that employees are the true source of added value and that there exists an implicit reciprocal relationship between employee and organization: that employees agree to invest their time and effort to further organizational goals in exchange for organizational commitment to treating them equitably with both recognition and respect. Korsgaard (1996), for example, maintains that the normative humanistic stance of an individual obligates others to adopt a similar stance. Similarly, Harvey (2001) argues that normative theories invoke an obligation to attend to the well-being and welfare of community members. It is therefore not surprising that recent approaches to humanistic management focus on building a community of persons embedded in an organizational culture that fosters the requisite character (Mele, 2003). The literature maintains that such approaches must take into account human needs, motivations, and the well-being of individuals.

Swanson and Holton (2001) argue that humanism is absolutely central to the HRD field with its core emphasis on the inner motivation of employees to develop themselves. Kramlinger and Huberty (1990) argue that the core assumption underpinning the humanistic approach is that learning occurs primarily through reflection on personal experience. They list the techniques of inductive discussion using the Socratic method, action planning, self-assessment, and guided reflection as forming the essence of a people-centered approach to HRD. Oh, what a beautiful world!

## The Real Nature of Organizations in Liberal Capitalist Society

Humanistic approaches promote a caring, considerate image of organizations amenable to employee concerns. By adopting developmental language, emphasis is placed on employee self-actualization and development, primarily for the individual's benefit (Guest, 1999). However, this person-centered view of HRD generally fails to make explicit the instrumental objective of increasing shareholder returns, profit, market share, and, dare we say it, maximizing employee productivity at minimum cost. Direct, indirect, and opportunity costs are incurred by all organizations in conducting HRD activities. Return on investment is a key concern for those charged with budget creation. In short, humanist approaches may mislead employees, and perhaps HRD professionals, by fostering the illusion that the needs of employees and organizations are always mutually inclusive. In an increasingly individualized and brutally competitive business world, a massive gulf exists between the potential of the humanistic "mutual gains enterprise" (Kochan & Osterman, 1994) and the mercenary "individualised corporation" (Ghoshal & Bartlett, 1998), many of which will never make it to the Fortune Best 100.

For today's educated workforce, in the developed world at least, it has become a case of substituting the old battle for decent working conditions and wages with the call for stimulating work and the opportunity to participate in and design their own destinies. The self-organizing-development aspect of HRD would appear to provide this substitute and explains, if in part, the appeal of humanistic approaches.

Many powerful forces influence an organization's ability to compete effectively; globalization, changes in political and geopolitical relationships, economic restructuring, and the transforming technologies of the information age are the principal forces shaping the modern business landscape (Wilson, 2000). Organizations are becoming leaner and meaner (Burke & Nelson, 1998), with the preferred tools of choice more often than not being downsizing, layoffs, outsourcing, plant closures, or relocations (Burke, 2002; Gowing, Kraft, & Quick, 1998). Stein (2001) notes that downsizing often fails to deliver on the vast expectations made of it and that it frequently results in reduced levels of productivity, trust, and morale among surviving employees. Uchitelle and Kleinfeld (1996) maintain that the social contract between employers and employees has effectively been cancelled, and a huge literature has emerged on the changing nature of the psychological contract. This poses some serious questions regarding the supposed morality of humanistic approaches that offer employees the illusion of security and certainty in rapidly changing, unpredictable economic circumstances. Consequently, it is arguable that while humanistic approaches might appear to yield favorable results in the short run, they are probably doomed in the long run.

## Ethics and the Organization

The dominance of humanistic approaches and the image that they present a softer, more responsive form of management contribute to the popular misconception that these approaches, by their nature, necessarily entail a relinquishing of managerial control. In reality, humanistic approaches are indicative of a modern, sophisticated, latently strategic approach to people management, designed to elicit proactive, self-motivated employee behavior. Alvesson and Deetz (1996, p. 192) argue that "objects of management control are decreasingly labor power and behavior and increasingly the mindpower and subjectivities of employees"—knowledge and intellectual capital. Weick (1979) argues that managerial work can be viewed as managing myths, images, symbols, and labels in a meaningful way to reinforce employees' understanding of organizational priorities. The role of the media in advancing the humanist agenda has also come under scrutiny. Deetz and McKinley (2000) argue that the acceptance and acquiescence by employees of corporate values is indicative of a broader media-constructed reality that is supportive of the values of corporate leaders. They argue that this reality facilitates a hegemonic ideology whereby the content of media outlets can be used to shape individual values and set the public agenda. Favorable portrayals of corporations in the media help in promoting both unitarist strategies and humanistic approaches in HRD, both of which exclude, conceal, or downplay any adverse social consequences of corporate activity.

On the surface, the adoption of humanistic approaches by organizations supports the view that organizations have a social agenda as well as an economic one. They present to employees the ethos and ideals of a nonprofit organization where individuals work together for the unitarist "good of all." Wilson (2000) argues that if the corporation is a social as distinct from a purely economic institution, then corporations should operate in a way that expresses not just economic values such as efficiency, productivity, economic value, and improved standards of material living, but a broader range of social values that reflect the prevailing societal ethos. While this is admirable, we may suggest that Wilson is somewhat lost in the humanistic forest here. The real test of the morality of an act is the intrinsic value of the results (Kagan, 1998), and there is as yet no ethical rug (Swanson, 2001) under which all the anomalies of the humanistic illusion can be swept. Outhwaite (1994) notes Kunneman's (1991) argument that recent moves toward workplace democracy may be something of a unitarist illusion. Similarly, O'Donnell (1999) exposes the myth of workplace democracy, stating:

> The role of communicative processes in formal organisations can . . . be analysed more closely if one represents the formal, juridically structured

framework of enterprises and state bureaucracies as a container into which communicative processes are squeezed in and dammed up. As soon as these threaten to become dysfunctional for the goals of the organisation, sanctions that are not communicatively criticisable can be brought into play [p. 258].

## Conclusion

The rhetoric of humanistic approaches to HRD, which espouses developmental ideals and supportive organizational structures focused on employee self-actualization, is not matched by organizational actions of compressed career progression pathways, tight budgetary constraints, and a market-driven economic philosophy.

There exists a real danger that HRD interventions will be co-opted by HR practitioners as effective tools in promoting unitarist ideologies in organizations, to the medium-term detriment of employees. The intrinsic demands of the performance paradigm are not compatible with humanistic approaches in HRD (Swanson & Holton, 2001). Professionals in HRD are not in the business of marketing illusions, and a modicum of realism is far better, and ethically superior, for both sides.

Gabriel (2001) suggests that there is a crisis in humanistic thinking, that there has been a floundering of critical imagination, and that modern theories do not strive to change the world or even to understand it but increasingly seek to deconstruct it, accepting without challenge the hegemonic agenda. Jeffcutt (1998, p. 107) notes, however, that "critical dialogue between the rationalist conventions of critical theory and the relativist subversions of poststructuralism describes a complex territory that is both ragged and contradictory." Humanistic approaches, however, which exist in this complex, ragged, and contradictory territory, continue to be too uncritically taken for granted by far too many theorists and practitioners. They do not tell the full story. HRD needs to be told explicitly as it is; the crisis for HRD is that it is not.

## References

Addesso, P. J. (1996). *Management would be easy—if it weren't for the people*. New York: AMACOM.

Aktouf, O. (1992). Management theories of organisations in the 1990s: Towards a critical radical humanism? *Academy of Management Review, 17*, 407–417.

Alvesson, M., & Deetz, S. (1996). Critical theory and postmodern approaches to organizational studies. In S. R. Clegg, C. Hardy, & W. R. Nord (Eds.), *Handbook of organization studies* (pp. 191–217). Thousand Oaks, CA: Sage.

Burke, R. J. (2002). Organizational transitions. In C. L. Cooper & R. J. Burke (Eds.), *The new world of work: Challenges and opportunities* (pp. 3–28). Oxford: Blackwell.

Burke, R. J., & Nelson, D. L. (1998). Mergers and acquisitions, downsizing and privatisations: A North American perspective. In M. K. Gowing, J. D. Kraft, & J. C. Quick (Eds.), *The new organizational reality: Downsizing, restructuring and revitalisation* (pp. 21–54). Washington, DC: American Psychological Association.

Deetz, S., & McKinley, E. G. (2000). Corporations, the media industry and society ethical imperatives and responsibilities. In K. F. Kersten & W. E. Biernatzki (Eds.), *Value and communication: Critical humanistic perspectives* (pp. 39–70). Cresskill, NJ: Hampton Press.

Fulmer, I. S., Gerhart, B., & Scott, K. S. (2003). Are the 100 best better? An empirical investigation of the relationship between being a "great place to work" and firm performance. *Personnel Psychology, 56,* 965–993.

Gabriel, Y. (2001). The state of critique in organizational theory. *Human Relations, 54* (1), 23–30.

Ghoshal, S., & Bartlett, C. A. (1998). *The individualized corporation.* London: Heinemann.

Gowing, M. K., Kraft, J. D., & Quick, J. C. (1998). Helping people and organizations deal with the impact of competitive change: An AT&T case study. In M. K. Gowing, J. D. Kraft, & J. C. Quick (Eds.), *The new organizational reality: Downsizing, restructuring and revitalisation* (pp. 77–98). Washington DC: American Psychological Association.

Guest, D. (1999). Human resource management—The worker's verdict. *Human Resource Management Journal, 9* (3), 5–25.

Harvey, M. (2001). The hidden force: A critique of normative approaches to business leadership. *Advanced Management Journal, 66* (4), 36–47.

Henderson, G. (1996). *Human relations issues in management.* Westport, CT: Quorum Books.

Huselid, M. A. (1995). The impact of human resource management practices on turnover, productivity, and corporate financial performance. *Academy of Management Journal, 38*(3), 635–672.

Jeffcutt, P. (1998). Making sense of management: Opening up some critical space. *Management Learning, 29* (1), 105–108.

Kagan, S. (1998). *Normative ethics.* Boulder, CO: Westview.

Knowles, M. S., Holton, E. F., & Swanson, R. A. (1998). *The adult learner,* (5th ed.). Houston: Gulf Publishing.

Kochan, T. A., & Osterman, P. (1994). *The mutual gains enterprise.* Boston: Harvard Business School Press.

Korsgaard, C. M. (1996). *The sources of relativity.* Cambridge: Cambridge University Press.

Kramlinger, T., & Huberty, T. (1990). Behaviorism versus humanism. *Training and Development Journal, 44* (12), 41–46.

Kruger, V. (1998). Total Quality Management and its humanistic orientation towards organizational analysis. *TQM Magazine, 10,* 293–302.

Kunneman, H. (1991). *Der Wahrheitstrichter: Habermas und die Postmoderne.* Frankfurt: Campus.

Mele, D. (2003). The challenge of humanistic management. *Journal of Business Ethics, 44* (1), 77–88.

O'Donnell, D. (1999). Habermas, critical theory and selves—Directed learning. *Journal of European Industrial Training, 23* (4/5), 251–258.

Outhwaite, W. (1994). *Habermas: A critical introduction.* Cambridge: Polity Press.

Schuster, F. E. (1998). *Employee-centered management: A strategy for high commitment and involvement.* Westport, CT: Quorum Books.

Stein, H. F. (2001). *Nothing personal, just business.* Westport, CT: Quorum Books.

Swanson, R.A. (2001). Human resource development and its underlying theory. *Human Resource Development International, 4* (3), 299–307.

Swanson, R. A., & Holton, E. F. (2001). *Foundations of human resource development.* San Francisco: Berrett-Koehler.

Uchitelle, L., & Kleinfeld, N. (1996, March 3). The downsizing of America. *New York Times,* p. 10.

Weick, K. (1979). Cognitive processes in organizations. *Research in Organizational Behavior, 1,* 41–74.

Wilson, I. (2000). *The new rules of corporate conduct.* Westport, CT: Quorum Books.

*David McGuire is a Fulbright Scholar in the Department of Human Resource Development, School of Education and Human Services, at Oakland University in Rochester Hills, Michigan.*

*Christine Cross is a lecturer in the Department of Personnel and Employment Relations, Kemmy Business School, at the University of Limerick in Castletroy, Limerick, Ireland.*

*David O'Donnell is the director of the Intellectual Capital Research Institute of Ireland in Ballyagran, Ireland.*

For bulk reprints of this article, please call (201) 748-8789.

# Mental Traps to Avoid While Interpreting Feedback: Insights from Administering Feedback to School Principals

*Neharika Vohra, Manjari Singh*

*This article summarizes our experiences in the counseling sessions that followed the administration of multifaceted feedback to 107 principals. The various responses displayed by the principals toward the feedback they received are discussed. The responses have been classified as those avoiding and denial at two levels (avoidance of the feedback received and denial in the process of interpretation), rationalization of the feedback received, superficiality in data interpretation, and unnatural behavioral manifestations on receiving the feedback such as overreaction and overdramatization, self-pity, and starting to feel unwell. Although these reactions might help the recipient avoid feeling anxious or upset about the feedback, these are also traps that stop the recipient from benefiting from the feedback. Knowledge of such reactions may help recipients of feedback to inoculate themselves against such traps and thus help them gain maximally from the feedback process.*

Feedback is the information people give to the role incumbent about the incumbent's performance outcomes, behavior patterns, competence, ideas, and actions. It has been claimed as motivating, satisfying, and a learning experience. Feedback received also helps to highlight areas of improvement and define self-concept (Shrauger & Schoeneman, 1979).

There are several steps in the feedback process: collecting, collating, receiving, and interpreting. The last two steps, receiving and interpreting, are crucial (Kluger & DeNisi, 1996). Most feedback can be rendered useless if adequate time is not spent in analyzing and interpreting it. The process of receiving feedback, not unlike when one looks into the mirror or hears one's own recorded voice, arouses all sorts of feelings: anxiety, fear, shame, satisfaction, and others. Most such feelings are difficult to confront and accept (Blanchard, 1998). Thus, people are known to unconsciously or consciously protect themselves against anxiety and awareness of threats by erecting mental blocks (Ilgen & Davis, 2000) known as psychological defenses (American Psychiatric Association, 1994).

Heads of any organization or institution are often in positions of unquestioned and unlimited power. Others in the organization shield their views from the organizational head, limiting access to feedback. Thus, they find the process of receiving, accepting, and interpreting feedback even more difficult (Rao, 2002) and are more likely to overcome their natural anxieties engendered in the process by erecting defenses. This article presents and discusses some reactions and their manifestations when 107 secondary school principals received multifaceted feedback in the course of a leadership development program in Ahmedabad, India.

We prepared a report comprising multifaceted feedback from students, teachers, parents, nonteaching staff, and members of management committee about the principals and gave it to each principal in a sealed envelope in the privacy of his or her room for perusal at any time (Singh & Vohra, in press). A worksheet designed for processing the feedback and preparing a developmental plan was also included in the packet. All principals were asked to interpret the data and prepare their developmental plan. After they had filed the developmental plan, they could voluntarily schedule personal meetings with us to discuss their feedback.

The typical and often repeated reactions of principals in the personal counseling sessions and within or outside classroom after receiving their feedback are schematically represented in Figure 1. The responses have been classified as those avoiding and denying feedback received at the level of the actual data and their interpretation, rationalization of the feedback received, superficial interpretation of data, and unnatural behavioral manifestations on receiving the feedback.

Knowledge of typical reactions to feedback can help the recipients of feedback become aware of their own behaviors and reactions. This awareness may allow them to go past their first and natural reactions and thus derive maximize benefit from the feedback process.

## Avoidance and Denial

In avoidance, the recipient of the feedback attempts to ignore or disbelieve what is presented in the feedback and believe that the opposite is the case (American Psychiatric Association, 1994). Such avoidance or denial can be manifested in the recipient's denying the feedback received and believing that the data that were collected were untrue or by avoiding reality and not attending to the information, or finding inappropriate benchmarks.

*Avoidance and Denial Evidenced in Disbelieving the Data.* Sometimes the principals avoided accepting their feedback by refusing to believe the giver and his or her intent or questioning the appropriateness of the chosen sample.

## Figure 1. A Schematic Representation of Reactions to Feedback

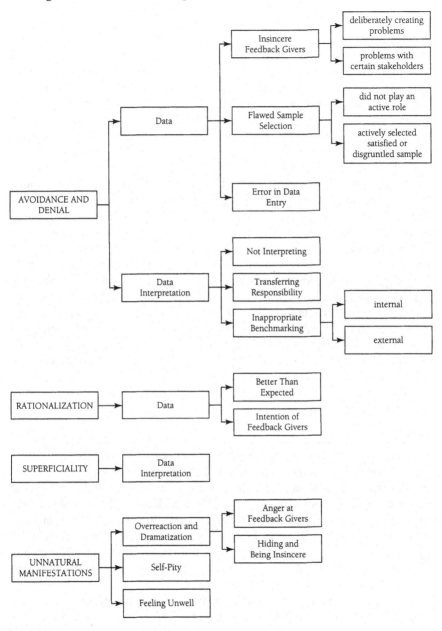

*Denial of Feedback Received from the Giver.* This denial can take two forms:

• Doubting the intent of the giver. Seeing their feedback, some principals believed that a conspiracy may have been hatched against them and thus say, "I think some individuals have given adverse remarks simply to create problems for me." Although it is possible that some respondents may have tried to slander the principal and hiding behind anonymity, experience has shown that very rarely is anonymous feedback used to be vengeful. Thus, thinking that the feedback received is a function of some individuals' hostility toward the giver is probably denial. However, if a recipient knows for certain that such an assertion is true, we suggest that "motivated" remarks should be discounted in the interpretation of the data.

• Believing only favorable feedback. It is not uncommon to hear variations of statements such as, "My teachers and students are good, but the parents and management committee are my bottleneck." It is important to use the opportunity offered by the feedback given to examine if the not-so-positive feedback that has been received is indicative of the current effectiveness of the incumbent's role with respect to the stakeholders. There is a possibility that the stakeholder group in question may not be helping the principal and he or she may in turn be not giving his or her best to the group. This cycle of events reinforces mutual negative expectations. Therefore, when several members of the same group give similar feedback, we suggest that rather than treating the group as problematic, the recipient carefully examine his or her behavior and discharge of roles with reference to that group and see what might be done to increase role effectiveness.

*Avoidance or Denial by Attributing It to Sample Selection.* This type of avoidance or denial has two forms:

• "I did not play any role in selection." Many principals were surprised at the feedback that they received. To avoid confronting the surprising information, some of them would say, "I did not play any role in selecting who the respondents should be, but I think my vice principal did not really understand the task." Rather than openly accepting the feedback, recipients make a self-justificatory attempt to claim that the feedback is a function of the respondents who were chosen rather than a function of reality. It is possible that the sample may not have been perfectly chosen, but the pertinent question for the recipient of the feedback is to look at the picture that is being presented by the randomly chosen sample.

• "I played an active role." Another similar way of justifying the feedback is to say that "it is positive because I told the vice principal to ensure none of the rebels were given the questionnaire" or "it is negative because I requested the vice principal to give the questionnaire to all the disgruntled teachers, parents, and students." If this is what a principal has really done, we suggest that all feedback be ignored because the principal has interfered with an important part of the process of collecting data, that is, randomization. Choosing the sample randomly makes it probable that the effect of any extreme responses or biases is cancelled out. Interfering with the choice of sample is most likely to give biased results. However, we are also conscious that this line of reasoning is used to deny unexpected feedback. Only the recipient of the feedback would know the truth and has to make an effort to move past self-defense and accept the reality.

*Avoidance or Denial in Attributing the Feedback to Mistakes in Data Entry.* Here, the response might be, "Are you sure you have scored this correctly? Where I most expected the responses to be positive, they are negative." Another commonly practiced technique for discounting the feedback is to disbelieve the messenger. However, it really does not help to shoot the bearer of bad news. If the feedback that has been received is the opposite of what was expected, it would be instructive to examine the reasons for this variance. Reversals of expected trends could indicate that the recipient was not able to read the signs and was not fully aware of the dynamics with the group in question or with respect to a certain situation. A close confidant may be able to help in deciphering such patterns.

**Avoidance While Interpreting the Feedback.** At the stage of interpretation of feedback, it was found that recipients displayed avoidance by simply not investing in the time to understand the feedback. In other cases, after interpretation, they looked for comparisons with other schools or avoided the feedback by holding others responsible for the feedback received.

*Being Cognitively Lazy and Not Investing in the Interpretation.* A detailed worksheet along with the feedback was given to the principals to help them analyze feedback. However, many were cognitively lazy and wanted us to interpret their feedback for them. Thus, they would say, "Here is my feedback; tell me what I should do now." It is true that in the beginning, it is difficult for many people to analyze large amounts of data. However, the recipient has to make an effort to examine, understand, live with, and internalize the data. Otherwise, the exercise of collecting and receiving feedback may become futile. The analysis and internalization of feedback help maximize the returns from the whole process.

*Transferring Responsibility for Feedback to Others.* Some of the principals looking at their feedback would say, "I am too good for my school. I think I must find another school where they will benefit from my capabilities." In this instance, the recipient thinks that the feedback is the way it is because of the people who gave the feedback. This is a classic case of avoidance and transferring of responsibility from self to others. This reaction helps the recipient avoid facing the reality, but also defeats the entire purpose of the feedback process. It is important to remember that the usefulness of feedback is dependent on the recipient's owning the feedback that he or she receives.

*Inappropriate Benchmarking.* This category encompasses looking for internal and external benchmarks.

In the category of looking for internal benchmarks, some principals will spend time looking at their feedback and then ask the innocuous-sounding question, "Don't you think this is how it should be?" as if seeking confirmation and certification of their performance. It is true that it would be good to know what the desired state is, but often the desired state is not uniform and applicable to all. The desired state is contingent on circumstances, skills, and the situation. For example, a school that attracts the best students because of its reputation needs to recruit very bright teachers, and the principal must find ways of doing that. The same may not be true for a semiurban school that has many students who are first-generation learners. In such a school, it would be desirable to find and recruit patient and caring teachers. The recipient has to assess the feedback in the light of the situation he or she works in. However, it is important to guard against defending the feedback as satisfactory by attributing it to circumstances. The recipient has to be honest and set high performance standards. A certificate by an outsider about the level of performance would be less useful than an honest self-certification of one's performance.

In looking for external benchmarks, many principals are keen to know the means and standard deviation for the various items as compared to other principals. They find it impossible or difficult to interpret their own feedback when they do not know how they have fared in comparison to other principals. It is common to use norms to compare one's own scores with the scores of others. However, norms are often computed for ability and personality measures. But feedback is the assessment of various groups based on their observations and experiences with the role incumbent and is not a measure of ability or personality. It is contextual and cannot be compared to the performance of others. Comparison of feedback with others defeats the purpose of giving and receiving multifaceted feedback.

The converse of this response is also common: "Do you think it is right to compare across cities and schools? In my situation, I have to face so many more difficulties." In addition to politely explaining that the comparison is being done by them, not us, we confirm that yes, it is not fair! Neither is it necessary to compare downward or upward to interpret the feedback. The recipient is the best judge of his or her situation and must interpret the feedback accordingly.

## Rationalizing and Finding Justification

These reactions display tendency to find reasons or excuses for feedback that was below expectations (American Psychiatric Association, 1994).

Sometimes the feedback is better than expected, and the recipient might say, "Though many scores are low, they are still much better than I expected." This comment is made often for part of rather than the entire feedback. Though it is advisable to examine the feedback in the context in which it was taken, it may be perfectly justified to say, "The feedback is better than I expected because I am going through a very bad patch at this time with respect to managing the nonteaching staff." However, it would also be wise to be warned against rationalization, that is, trying to justify or explain negative feedback. Rationalizing is a perfectly fair self-preservation mechanism until it is done in a manner that you may not be turning a blind eye to something that may be of benefit in the long run.

Another common response was trying to understand the intention of the feedback givers: "I can figure out who would have said this. Let me tell you the intention behind this." Many principals insisted on trying to locate the sources of the feedback (an example of rationalization). The feedback is designed to provide an overall picture of how others perceive the recipient and assess his or her effectiveness. Rationalizing the feedback in this manner is a fallacy of relevance; the source has nothing to do with whether the feedback is accurate. If recipients convince themselves that the poor feedback is because of a fault or problem with the source, they may protect their self-image, but they will not benefit from the feedback process. In addition, if this investigation becomes known to the givers of the feedback, they may feel victimized. In this situation, the feedback process would lose credibility, and the recipient would never be able to repeat this process for self or other groups.

## Superficiality

This is the tendency to gloss over subtle aspects of the feedback and pay attention only to that which is expected and obvious.

Many principals take a quick look at the feedback and happily conclude, "My feedback is wonderful. I do not need to spend any time exploring it." Although self-congratulation is a positive behavior, superficial contentment should not be used as a mechanism to escape reality. We have often found that the recipient glosses over the nuances contained in the feedback. Maximum benefit can be gained by a detailed examination of the data and the context from which they derive. Extremely positive feedback may also not be representative of reality. Stakeholders may have given a socially desirable (that is, very positive) response because they believed that that was expected of them.

## Unnatural Manifestations

These exaggerated physical and mental reactions to feedback take several forms.

*Overreaction and Dramatization.* Many of us are given to dramatization and overreacting to negative feedback as a means to hide our real feelings. We have frequently encountered reactions such as, "I am shocked at what the parents and students have said. I will never be able to love or trust them again."

Such a response is not constructive for at least two reasons. First, if it were made public, such a sentiment would seriously undermine any future attempts at eliciting feedback. Second, the reaction does not represent an attempt to evaluate the data seriously.

*Hiding and Being Insincere.* Some principals react to negative or not-so-positive feedback by completely hiding it and being insincere. They tell all others that their feedback was wonderful and either how glad they were about it or how they did not really care about it. Such insincerity is disruptive to self and renders the feedback process completely useless for the recipient. Also, those who gave candid feedback feel cheated when they witness such behavior of the recipient. They might feel it is futile to give feedback to this person if he or she is not even going to look at. They would rarely give honest feedback in a repetition of such an exercise.

*Engaging in Self-Pity.* In some cases, there are responses such as, "I feel good that I got good feedback despite the fact that I have so many hurdles to overcome in my school." This line of thought is nothing but self-pity. It is a way to avoid spending time thinking about the details of the feedback. Focusing on the hurdles or difficulties of the job shifts the focus from the feedback to self. Self-pity blocks the ability to use feedback for improvement.

It is also not uncommon to hear variations of this statement: "Management gives good feedback but not good infrastructure." This is again an instance of not focusing on the feedback. The recipient needs to realize that the group that has given the feedback understands the problems the role incumbent faces but still appreciates the work done.

*Feeling Unwell.* Some principals manifested physical reactions, such as stomach cramps, after receiving the feedback. These might be because the recipient does not accept his or her feelings about the feedback and is trying to suppress them. For such individuals, accepting the feedback and the feelings that it engenders is important rather than bottling up those reactions. Acceptance is the basis of honest analysis of the feedback.

## Conclusion

We encountered all of the classic forms of resistance (ignoring and denial, repression, and rationalization) to negative information in the responses of the principals. These varied forms of resistance were used to shift the focus away from the self and on to those giving the feedback, the medium, or the instrument. The price of keeping the ego intact is the missed opportunity of gaining from the feedback (Audia & Locke, 2003).

Those giving the feedback also monitor the behavior of the recipient after the exercise is complete. How the recipient reacts to the feedback—with maturity, anger, feelings of vindication, or retribution—determines the subsequent behavior of the givers of feedback. Thus, if the recipients wish to create a culture of honesty and openness, they must consciously focus on how they react to the received feedback (Ashford & Tsui, 1991).

It is important to emphasize that the principals or heads of an organization are not unique in falling prey to these traps and displaying such reactions. We expect that anyone receiving comprehensive feedback, especially if it is for the first time, might have the same reactions.

## References

American Psychiatric Association. (1994). *Diagnostic and statistical manual of mental disorders* (4th rev. ed.). Washington DC: Author.

Ashford, S. J., & Tsui, A. S. (1991). Self-regulation for managerial effectiveness: The role of active feedback seeking. *Academy of Management Journal, 34,* 251–280.

Audia, P. G., & Locke, E. A. (2003). Benefiting from negative feedback. *Human Resource Management Review, 13,* 631–646.

Blanchard, K. (1998). Giving and receiving feedback. *Executive Excellence, 15* (10), 8.

Ilgen, D. R., & Davis, C. A. (2000). Bearing bad news: Reactions to negative performance feedback. *Applied Psychology: An International Review, 49* (3), 550–565.

Kluger, A. N., & DeNisi, A. (1996). The effects of feedback interventions on performance: A historical review, a meta analysis, and a preliminary feedback intervention theory. *Psychological Bulletin, 119,* 254–284.

Rao, T. V. (2002). The power of 360 degree feedback. In T. V. Rao, G. Mahapatra, R. Rao, R., & N. Chawla (Eds.), *360 degree feedback and performance management system* (Vol. 2, pp. 43–50). New Delhi: Excel Books.

Shrauger, J. S., & Schoeneman, T. J. (1979). Symbolic interactionist view of self-concept: Through the looking glass darkly. *Psychological Bulletin, 86,* 549–573.

Singh, M., & Vohra, N. (in press). Multifaceted feedback for organizational heads for self and organizational development: Experiences of school principals. *International Journal of Training and Development.*

*Neharika Vohra is associate professor in the Organizational Behavior Area at the Indian Institute of Management, Ahmedabad, India.*

*Manjari Singh is assistant professor in the Personnel and Industrial Relations Area at the Indian Institute of Management, Ahmedabad, India.*

# REVIEW

*Networks in the Knowledge Economy,* edited by R. Cross, A. Parker, and L. Sasson. New York: Oxford University Press, 2003. 349 pages. $39.95 (hardcover).

*Networks in the Knowledge Economy* is a collection of previously published articles on the development of social network analysis as an analytical tool and an intervention process for organizational performance improvement. The collection is for scholars and practitioners interested in understanding or managing the informal relationships that arise in organizations. It is not for experienced social network analysis professionals. Human resource development (HRD) professionals interested in new ways of looking at socialization, organizational learning, learning networks, collaboration, innovation diffusion, organizing for performance, knowledge sharing, and organizational culture will find this book very useful and even thought provoking. It offers conceptual understanding by illuminating how different informal network structures can shape performance outcomes, and it provides managers with data and guidelines that can help them shape the informal structures that can emerge when people work together. It is time for HRD scholars and practitioners to consider using social network analysis as a tool and method to understand, evaluate, or assess informal structures in organizations.

Social network analysis illuminates the informal networks of employees that knowledge-dependent organizations rely on, and helps managers support the work of these collaborations. "While such networks are not generally found on any formal organization charts, they frequently can be sources of both strategic and operational success for an organization" (p. 4).

This book describes the historical development and relevance of social network analysis in easy-to-understand terms. Most of the chapters of the book can be easily absorbed by people unfamiliar with social network analysis methods, history, and practices. Both HRD researchers and practitioners will find it very useful for the assessment of, research on, and practice of building informal social networks to contribute to organizational performance. The contributors to this edited volume are drawn from the disciplines of sociology and management, and manuscripts were initially published in a wide range of journals, including the *American Journal of Sociology, Organization Dynamics, Harvard Business Review,* the *California Management Review,* and *New Yorker.*

From this list, one can glean that the expected audience includes researchers, executives, and other reflective practitioners. Is it for HRD? You bet. Not only does the book present foundational, renowned scholarship about the role of social networks at work (examples are Mark Granovetter's "Strength of Weak Ties," David Krackhardt and Jeffrey Hanson's "Informal Networks: The Company Behind the Chart," and Daniel Brass's "A Social Network Perspective on Human Resources Management"), but it also includes practitioner-focused prescriptions about how to understand, develop, and manage these networks in the work context (examples are Malcolm Gladwell's "Designs for Working" and Rob Cross, Stephen Borgatti, and Andrew Parker's "Making Invisible Work Visible"). In other words, this book presents both the scholarship on and practice of social networks in terms relevant to HRD professionals.

The introduction is dedicated to providing the layperson with an understanding of the power of social network analysis in easy-to-understand language. In addition, the introduction clearly aims to convince readers that social network analysis is a necessary tool for those responsible for developing and managing groups of people in the work context. The editors note, "Most work of importance is heavily reliant on informal networks of employees within organizations" (pp. 3–4), and that social network analysis "provides an important means of assessing and promoting collaboration in strategically important groups" (p. 4). The introduction does a nice job at answering the "what" and "so what" of informal networks and social network analysis as the tool to examine them.

The book has three parts. Part One, "Social Networks as Important Individual and Organizational Assets," presents three historical and seminal works of social network literature by Ronald Burt, James S. Coleman, and David Krackhardt. These authors are arguably in the top tier of scholars who focus on informal social networks. Burt offers a conceptual chapter on understanding how social networks cause what economists term imperfect competition. Unlike the rest of the chapters, which are relatively easy to absorb even without previous social network analysis knowledge, Burt's piece is a bit more challenging. He provides a rich (but somewhat difficult to read and absorb) tapestry of social network concepts, consequences, and benefits. The time needed to process this rich information will pay off in terms of the depth of understanding readers will gain about how social networks can be an individual asset in a variety of ways and for a variety of reasons.

Chapters by Coleman and Krackhardt round out Part One. Coleman's seminal piece explains how social networks affect a person's knowledge, skills, and abilities. In other words, Coleman argues, social capital shapes human capital. This position has interesting implications for HRD professionals interested in human capital, as well as for scholars and practitioners interested in diversity. Like Burt's, this is a conceptual piece that offers readers a foundation of understanding the sociological perspective.

Krackhardt's chapter, originally published in 1992, set off a debate in the sociological literature about the value of strong versus weak ties, with *ties* defined as the link between two people. Previous research had suggested that weakly connected individuals offer each other important relational gifts. In part, Krackhardt was responding to Mark Granovetter's 1973 "strength of weak tie" argument. Krackhardt poked at the research on weak ties by arguing that measuring tie strength is problematic, and accounting for the psychological implications of tie strength is very important (something that Granovetter did not address). This chapter offers the HRD professional who is unversed in social network jargon a clear primer on social network analysis and the components of measuring the ties between people. Krackhardt argues that strong ties are more important than weak ties for certain types of performance and organizational goals. To make his argument explicit, he offers a case study of a unionization attempt at a Silicon Valley company. The case study offers provocative insights for HRD professionals interested in issues around collective action and unionizing in a business context.

The five chapters in Part Two, "Social Network Implications for Knowledge Creation and Sharing," represent a wide diversity of audience and intent. Beginning with Mark Granovetter's seminal piece already described, Part Two also offers two chapters from Malcolm Gladwell that were originally published in the *New Yorker*. The other two chapters are by Everett Rogers, on diffusion networks, and by Rob Cross et al., on how to support optimal social networks for certain types of performance objectives. The purpose of these five articles seems to be to illuminate, from different perspectives and for different audiences, the consequences of informal networks on how knowledge is created and shared. For the HRD professional, these chapters clearly and concisely connect knowledge creation and knowledge sharing with the study and practice of social networks. They provide a deep understanding of how networks shape knowledge flow between people, as well as how networks can shape the type of knowledge that is generated by a group of people.

Finally, Part Three, "Managerial Implications of Social Networks in Organizations," provides the practice- or intervention-focused literature on social networks for the manager or HRD practitioner interested in shaping certain network formations to meet performance objectives. Many of these chapters are written by notable social network analysis scholars who have moved their research from the conceptual and abstract and into the real world of organizational action. David Krackhardt and Jeffrey Hanson, Rob Cross and Andrew Prusak, Rob Cross, Stephen Borgatti, and Andrew Parker, Daniel Brass, and David Krackhardt (1994) present an interesting blend of older and newer influences on using social network analysis as an intervention tool. They suggest that social network analysis can support strategic collaboration, further human resource management practices, identify optimal or detrimental structures to organizational objectives, and identify the main informal influencers within the formal organizational structure. All of these topics continue to be of interest to many HRD professionals, and reading these chapters provides an interesting alternative perspective from the more traditional perspective found in HRD journals.

This edited book has a clear goal of raising awareness of the value and strength of social network analysis in today's knowledge economy. The chapters complement that focus and offer novice readers a foundation for understanding and the impetus for future exploration. The book is not for experienced social network analysis scholars and practitioners, mainly because they have undoubtedly already read these articles when they were originally published. *Networks in the Knowledge Economy* is directed at those new to social network analysis, and, I believe, HRD professionals seeking new ways to understand collaboration, knowledge sharing, and information flow in organizational contexts. The book editors have succeeded in piecing together a strong argument for social network analysis and blending together a diverse array of scholarship to prove their point.

REVIEWED BY
JULIA STORBERG-WALKER
NORTH CAROLINA STATE UNIVERSITY
RALEIGH, NORTH CAROLINA

For bulk reprints of this article, please call (201) 748-8789.

*Human Resource Development Quarterly* is a publication sponsored by the American Society for Training and Development and the Academy of Human Resource Development. It provides a central focus for research on human resource development issues as well as the means for disseminating such research. *HRDQ* recognizes the interdisciplinary nature of the HRD field and brings together relevant research from the related fields, such as economics, education, management, and psychology. It provides an important link in the application of theory and research to HRD practice.

In general, *HRDQ* publishes scholarly work that addresses the theoretical foundations of HRD, HRD research, and evaluation of HRD practices. Articles concerned solely with the practice of HRD are not within the scope of this journal but may be more appropriate for practitioner-oriented publications such as *Training and Development Magazine*.

Authors may contribute to *HRDQ* by submitting manuscripts for peer review, for the nonrefereed forum section, and for the media reviews section.

## Manuscripts for Peer Review

Manuscripts submitted for review undergo a blind peer-review process. Manuscripts are initially evaluated based on appropriateness of content and style. Appropriate manuscripts are then reviewed by three or more reviewers. Authors are informed about the results of the review through a letter from the editor and associate editor, usually within two months. Authors are also provided copies of the reviewers' comments. Manuscripts should be prepared for review in accordance with the following criteria:

- Submit two copies of the manuscript, including all graphics, figures, and tables in camera-ready form. Authors should submit a computer file in Word (.doc) or Rich Text Format (.rtf) at this time.
- Adhere to the language and style guidelines as presented in the *Publication Manual of the American Psychological Association* (5th ed.). Double-space the entire manuscript. Margins should be at least one inch wide, with no more than 250 words per page. Use 12-point type size.
- Submit the manuscript on 8½" × 11" or A4 size paper. It should be fifteen to twenty-five pages long, including references, tables and figures, and an abstract of 100 to 150 words.
- Provide a cover letter stating that the manuscript has not already been published and that it is not being considered for publication elsewhere.
- Include a title page with complete name(s) and address(es) of author(s). The first page of the text should have the title only. Subsequent pages should have a running head of the title. No author identification should appear whatsoever in the text. Include a separate page with a biography of the author(s).
- Use nondiscriminatory language throughout the text.

Email manuscripts for review to Darlene Russ-Eft (zmresearch@aol.com) or Laura Boehme (boehmel@onid.orst.edu). Hard-copy manuscripts can be sent to Editor, *HRDQ*, Oregon State University, School of Education, 421 Education Hall, Corvallis, OR 97331.

## Forum Section

The forum section, the nonrefereed section of *HRDQ*, provides a way to present ideas or issues related to the human resource development field, differing perspectives on specific topics, and reactions to previously published articles. As suggested by its name, the forum section is meant to encourage open discourse among scholars, who may not necessarily share the same point of view on a topic. The field as a whole should be enlivened by the varying opinions presented in forum articles. In their own limited way, forum articles often make contributions to the HRD literature, if only by the scholarly interactions that they produce as a result. Established researchers, graduate students, and senior practitioners in particular are encouraged to submit forum manuscripts. In practice, the forum section has proven an excellent way for authors to be published in *HRDQ* for the first time. Forum manuscripts should be prepared in accordance with the following criteria:

- Submit two copies of the manuscript, including all graphics, figures, and tables in camera-ready form. Authors should submit a computer file in Word (.doc) or Rich Text Format (.rtf) at this time.
- Adhere to the language and style guidelines as presented in the *Publication Manual of the American Psychological Association* (5th ed.). Double-space the entire manuscript. Margins should be at least one inch wide, with no more than 250 words per page. Use 12-point type size.
- Submit the manuscript on 8½" × 11" or A4 size paper. It should be five to seven pages long, including references, tables, and figures.
- Indicate author's opinions where appropriate.

Submit forum manuscripts to Darlene Russ-Eft, Editor, *HRDQ*, Oregon State University, School of Education, 421 Education Hall, Corvallis, OR 97331 (email: zmresearch@aol.com).

## Media Review Section

The media review section of *HRDQ* provides a way to critique books, visual media, and computer software related to the human resource development field. The scholarly emphasis requires authors to have some understanding of the theoretical and practical context of the item being reviewed. In this way, the media reviews themselves can be expected to make meaningful contributions to the literature.

Media reviews can be of two types: single item or multi-item. Single-item reviews focus on one item that has recently become available. The copyright date should be within two years of the probable publication date of the review. Multi-item reviews focus on two or more items that address similar topics, issues, or lines of reasoning. One of the items should have a recent copyright date. Reviews of this type should seek to compare and contrast the items based on their perspectives, emphases, and assumptions, among other categories. Media review manuscripts should be prepared in accordance with the following criteria:

- Submit two copies of the manuscript. Authors should submit a computer file in Word (.doc) or Rich Text Format (.rtf) at this time.
- Adhere to the language and style guidelines as presented in the *Publication Manual of the American Psychological Association* (5th ed.). Double-space the entire manuscript. Margins should be at least one inch wide, with no more than 250 words per page. Use 12-point type size.
- Submit the manuscript on 8½" × 11" or A4 size paper. It should be five to seven pages long, including references.
- Provide the complete citation at the beginning of the manuscript, including the ISBN number.
- Describe the purpose of the item as stated or inferred by the author. Describe the content and structure of the item. Identify the primary and secondary audiences.
- Discuss the context, theoretical bases, or unique perspectives of the item, emphasizing its relationship to the human resource development field.
- Evaluate the contributions and weaknesses of the item in terms that are relevant to HRD researchers and senior practitioners.

Submit media review manuscripts to Timothy G. Hatcher, Associate Editor, *HRDQ*, Training & Development and Adult Education, 310M Poe Hall, North Carolina State University, Raleigh, NC 27695.

## Publication Process

Once a manuscript is accepted for publication, authors are required to provide a computer file of the complete manuscript. Authors are also asked to sign a letter of agreement granting the publisher the right to copyedit, publish, and copyright the material. The editor is responsible for reviewing the copyediting and for proofreading each issue, and will only contact authors if clarification is required. Copyedited manuscripts will not be returned to authors. Authors must ensure the accuracy of all statements—particularly data, quotations, and references—before submitting manuscripts. Authors will receive complimentary copies of the completed journal issue.

Authors requiring information about a manuscript under review should e-mail the managing editor, Laura Boehme, at boehmel@onid.orst.edu. All other official submission and editorial correspondence should be mailed to Darlene Russ-Eft, Editor, *HRDQ*, Oregon State University, School of Education, 421 Education Hall, Corvallis, OR 97331 (email: zmresearch@aol.com).

Sam Adams
*DeVry University*

Sonia Agut
*University of Murcia*

David Antonioni
*University of Wisconsin, Madison*

Susan Awbrey
*Oakland University*

Timothy T. Baldwin
*Indiana University*

Kenneth Bartlett
*University of Minnesota*

Reid Bates
*Louisiana State University*

Alexandra Bell
*University of Connecticut*

John Benson
*University of Melbourne*

Laura Bierema
*University of Georgia*

Paul Brauchle
*Illinois State University*

Ann K. Brooks
*University of Texas, Austin*

Celina Byers
*Oakland University*

Jamie Callahan
*Texas A&M University*

Shani Carter
*Rhode Island College*

Michael Cassidy
*Marymount University*

Melissa Cefkin
*Institute for Research on Learning*

Hsin-Chih Chen

Yuh Jia Chen
*Mid Tennessee State University*

Thomas Chermack

Eunsang Cho
*Korea Research Institute for Vocational Education & Training*

Alan Clardy
*Towson University*

Debra J. Cohen
*George Washington University*

Sharon Confessore
*Kaiser Permanente*

Maria Cseh
*Oakland University*

Barbara Daley
*University of Wisconsin-Milwaukee*

Jan De Jong
*Utrecht University*

Carol Decker
*Lincoln Memorial University*

Phillip J. Decker
*University of Houston*

Jennifer Dewey
*North Central Regional Education Laboratory*

Robert Dilworth
*Virginia Commonwealth University*

Sharon K. Drake
*Iowa State University*

Andrea Ellinger
*University of Alabama*

Michael Enos
*Clark/Bardes Consulting*

Kevin J. Freer
*Lucent Technologies*

Jo Gallagher
*Florida International University*

Sue Gallagher
*Miami Cerebral Palsy Services*

Brenda S. Gardner
*Xavier University*

Jerry Gilley
*Colorado State University*

Robert T. Golembiewski
*University of Georgia*

Thomas D. Gougeon
*University of Calgary*

Rosa Grau Gumbau
*Jaume University*

Paul J. Guglielmino
*Florida Atlantic University*

Lynn Harland
*University of Nebraska, Omaha*

Clark Hickman
*University of Missouri, St. Louis*

Barbara Hinton
*University of Arkansas*

Linda M. Hite
*Indiana-Purdue University*

Courtney Holladay
*Rice University*

Elwood Holton III
*Louisiana State University*

Barry-Craig P. Johansen
*University of Minnesota*

James R. Johnson
*Purdue University, Calumet*

Scott D. Johnson
*University of Illinois*

William M. Kahnweiler
*Georgia State University*

Roger Kaufman
*Florida State University*

Marijke Kehrhahn
*University of Connecticut*

Scott Keller
*Michigan State University*

Hye Shin Kim
*University of Delaware*

Nell Kimberley
*Monash University*

Howard Klein
*The Ohio State University*

Judith Kolb
*Pennsylvania State University*

Constantine Kontoghiorghes
*Cyprus International Institute of Management*

Sharon Korth
*Xavier University*

Kenneth A. Kovach
*George Mason University*

K. Peter Kuchinke
*University of Illinois*

Joseph Lapides
*University of Michigan*

Chan Lee
*Ohio State University*

Monica Lee
Lancaster University

Sharon Leiba-O'Sullivan
University of Ottawa

Michael P. Leimbach
Wilson Learning Corporation

Margaret C. Lohman
Penn State University, Harrisburg

Diannah Lowry
Flinders University

Germain D. Ludwig
Palm Beach Atlantic College

Susan Lynham
Texas A & M University

Susan Madsen
Utah Valley State College

Svjetlana Madzar
Gustavus Adolphus College

Victoria J. Marsick
Columbia University, Teachers College

Joseph Martelli
University of Findlay

Jennifer Martineau
Center for Creative Leadership

Joseph Martocchio
University of Illinois

Morgan W. McCall Jr.
University of Southern California

Timothy McClernon
People Architects, Inc.

Kimberly S. McDonald
Indiana-Purdue University

Gary McLean
University of Minnesota

Catherine Monaghan
University of Georgia

Max U. Montesino
Indiana–Purdue University

Hiromitsu Muta
Tokyo Institute of Technology

Frederick M. Nafukho
University of Arkansas

Sharon Naquin
Louisiana State University

Teresa M. Palmer
Illinois State University

Rob Poell
Tilburg University

Janet Polach
University of Minnesota

Toni Powell
Barry University

Hallie Preskill
University of New Mexico

J. Bruce Prince
Kansas State University

Kevin Quinlan
Nova Scotia Community College

Thomas Reio Jr.
University of Louisville

Peter J. Robertson
University of Southern California

William J. Rothwell
Pennsylvania State University

Robert Rowden
Brenau University

Wendy Ruona
University of Georgia

Eugene Sadler-Smith
University of Plymouth

Eduardo Salas
University of Central Florida

Soyeon Shim
University of Arizona

Thomas Shindell
Texas State Auditor's Office

Gilbert B. Siegel
University of Southern California

Sununta Siengthai
Asian Institute of Technology

Mark Skillings
Ohio State University

Catherine M. Sleezer
Oklahoma State University

Douglas H. Smith
Florida International University

Regina Smith
Portland State University

James Tan
University of Wisconsin, Stout

Thomas Li-Ping Tang
Middle Tennessee State University

Kecia Thomas
University of Georgia

Peg Thoms
Penn State Erie

Richard Torraco
University of Nebraska

Charles M. Vance
Loyola Marymount University

Mary Vielhaber
Eastern Michigan University

Janine Waclawski
Pepsi-Cola Company

Lori Wallace
University of Manitoba

John Walton
London Guildhall University

David Wan Wai Tai
National University of Singapore

Greg Wang
James Madison University

Karen E. Watkins
University of Georgia

Ryan Watkins
Nova University

Rose Mary Wentling
University of Illinois

Jon M. Werner
University of Wisconsin-Whitewater

Charles S. White
University of Tennessee, Chattanooga

Saundra Williams
North Carolina State University

JoAnne Willment
University of Calgary

Ida Wognum
University of Twente

Jean Woodall
Oxford Brookes University

Michael Workman
Florida State University

Phillip C. Wright
Hong Kong Baptist University

Lyle Yorks
Columbia University, Teachers College

# AHRD
## Academy of Human Resource Development
*Leading Human Resource Development Through Research*

The Academy of Human Resource Development (AHRD) is a global organization made up of, governed by, and created for the human resource development (HRD) scholarly community of academics and reflective practitioners. The Academy was formed to encourage systematic study of human resource development theories, processes, and practices; to disseminate information about HRD; to encourage the application of HRD research findings; and to provide opportunities for social interaction among individuals with scholarly and professional interests in HRD from multiple disciplines and from across the globe.

AHRD membership includes a subscription to *HRDQ*. A partial list of other benefits includes (1) membership in the only global organization dedicated to advancing the HRD profession through research, (2) annual research conference with full proceedings of research papers (900 pages), (3) reduced prices on professional books, (4) subscription to the *Forum,* the academy newsletter, and (5) research partnering, funding, and publishing opportunities.

Academy of Human Resource Development
College of Technology
Bowling Green State University
Bowling Green, Ohio 43403–0301

Phone:   419.372.9155
Fax:      419.372.8385
E-mail:   office@ahrd.org
Web site: www.ahrd.org